JOURNEY
TO
JOY

From Grief
to Inner Peace:
Embracing Life
After Loss

ANITA ALBRIGHT

Dedication

I dedicate this book to my inspiration and daughter, Bonnie Jeanne Albright, my brother, my mother, my father, my grandmothers, my grandfathers, my ancestors, and all those in the celestial realms who lit my path and guided me in the writing of this book.

My Intention

I am passionate about listening to people's stories and asking them questions about their experiences. If their story resonates with me, I often say, "You need to write a book!" I must have said this to my husband, John, a thousand times, only to realize that he had no interest in doing so.

What I discovered was that I was the one who needed to write the book. My purpose in writing this book is to inspire myself and others to remain focused on life's joyful journey despite the challenges of grief and loss. Living according to my highest vision taught me the importance of doing the right thing, being present, taking responsibility, speaking my truth, and following my inner guidance. I have also gained valuable insights from my experiences, especially those that didn't work. I trust that this book will positively impact its readers.

CONTENTS

"Attitude determines the quality of the outcome."

—John Albright, Sr.

Healing a Parent's Heart

waves of the light pulse
through the body
Feel it, the heart, the beat
Open and open and open.
Inhaling each breath,
Going deeper and deeper and deeper.
Exhaling . . . pain, grief, and sorrow
intense energy
in every cell, making new
Life again!
healing
lighting on the path
following the dots, finding the way.
Ease and grace! Freedom!
Move again up into the light.
Remember! True reality! Beauty, power, love, and truth!
Create, nurture, laugh, sing, and dance . . . tell the truth.
Empowered! The power releases, changing and shifting.

PREFACE

THE MAGIC OF WRITING

Writing is magic, better than a fairy godmother. With the stroke of a pen, I can release an emotion. Voilà! In writing, anger, frustration, fears, sadness, and joy are whooshed into the universe. Truths are revealed. I see things anew. It moves me to another level of myself, and I am transformed.

I first discovered the magic in writing when I was in sixth grade. My teacher, Sister Mary Edmund, asked the class to write a poem about someone significant to us. *"I'll write about my dear grandmother,"* I thought. Immediately, my grandmother came to my mind. A deep emotion rushed forth like a geyser upon its first release. I had struck oil, and all my feelings released the love I was holding inside.

My grandmother, Antonina (Anna) who I am named after, lived from 1885-1959. She was born in Italy and came to America via Ellis Island. I only knew her eight years but that was more than enough time for her to leave a lasting impression on me that held for my lifetime. I don't know much about her history, but I do know about her through my experience of her which left me with an eternal connection with her even after she left this Earth. She had a sparkle about her that made it fun for me to be with her. I adored her. My mother carried her essence and so do I.

Being the daughter of two immigrants, my mom kept her Italian culture while assimilating into American ways. She wanted her children to be American. She didn't want us ostracized because of our nationality.

In the winter of third grade, my mom left to pick up some bread at the corner store. I was lying on the sofa reading my book. I was alone, and a loud ring jolted me upright. I sprang to the phone. It was my aunt. She was in a panic. "I need to speak to your mother!"

"She's not here," I told her. "What's going on?"

"No, no, get your neighbor. No, no, go next door, go to Mrs. Brohawn's."

Frantically, I dropped the phone and ran next door. Mrs. Brohawn ran with me to my house, and I handed her the phone. My aunt spoke to her.

"So, what's going on?" I asked.

"I can't tell you. I must speak with your mother first."

This was my world. No one told children anything. I lived in a world of secrets, the adage being "children should be seen but not heard." Welcome to my world; maybe that's why I like to write. I want to do all the talking. Finally, Mrs. Brohawn told my mother. At last, my mother told me, and I cried and cried a river of tears. My grandmother was dead.

My grandmother, through her love, made me feel cherished and appreciated. She was the love of my life. During my visits with her, we played cards, hide and seek, and ate popcorn. She let me brush her long white hair and braid it. Just the way she looked at me told me she loved me dearly. She never said a cross word to me, and her words were always gentle and loving. She saw beauty in everybody and everything. I think she, indeed, was an angel.

Because of the travel distance and other parental reasons, I was not allowed to take time off school to attend the funeral and participate in the memorial activities. My parents were gone for a week. Bernice stayed with us: my older brother, my younger sister and myself. Bernice told us many stories and made us the best fried chicken. Yet all the while, my mind wandered, my heart yearned, and I was miserable. I was so angry at my parents. Didn't they know I had feelings too?

Frustrated and full of grief, I had no one with whom I could confide my loss. I carried a heavy heart filled with great sadness like a 50-pound dead weight. Upon my parents' return, my mother said, "Anita, put a smile on your face."

Thinking back, I was in sixth grade when I was given a significant personal writing assignment. I wrote a poem about my beloved grandmother. I did not struggle with it. It flowed forth, rhyme and all. I earned an "A" on that poem. I shared that poem with my classmates and my parents. A new feeling came over me. I smiled from the inside out

Thus began my relationship with the magic of writing. Over the years, I've found that when I'm struggling with an issue, I have kept many journals. I sit down, and the words flow out of me, and I feel new and renewed. Insight and new perspectives appear like magic. This is how this book came to be.

INTRODUCTION

This book chronicles my journey through loss and grief and the transformation that emerged. I hope it serves as a beacon of light for anyone facing life's challenges. May it inspire you to recognize, release and rediscover the wellspring of joy that lies within.

A traumatic and significant life event in 2016 led me on a path to personal growth and transformation. This event reshaped my understanding of the world, turning my beliefs inside out and upside down. It gave me new eyes. With a fresh perspective, I began to perceive and engage with life as a new person.

> *I finally persuaded my mind that it had no choice but to let go.*

Since my daughter Bonnie's passing, my life has been reorganizing. My heart was open, but my mind clung to patterns before 6/20/2016. I could not live with this internal conflict and be true to myself. As I gained clarity on what I needed to release, I opened to something far more meaningful than my mind had previously imagined. I had no choice but to change my thinking. I shifted my focus to what brought me joy. At first, it seemed radical, but eventually, it felt fitting.

My Path of Joy

"My Path of Joy" is a transformative journey centered around discovering and nurturing inner joy. Does this bring me joy? Is my heart guiding me? These questions serve as my guiding compass, inspiring and influencing my choices and actions while empowering me. This path is not limited to me alone—it is open to anyone and everyone, transcending the boundaries of groups, systems, or religions. It encompasses positivity, fulfillment, and alignment with a higher purpose, making it deeply meaningful and empowering for all. Each person's path toward joy manifests uniquely.

My journey involves acknowledging life's eternal nature and transcendence of death. I understand that our higher consciousness continues to exist even after the physical body is gone. This realization strengthens my belief in the omnipresence of my beloved daughter, Bonnie, who exists everywhere and in everything. Through "My Path to Joy," my work focuses on love, truth, and what life presents to me. I am retraining my capacities of body, mind and heart to express kindness, compassion and understanding in my world, so heaven and earth connect seamlessly.

Recognizing the Divine presence in all creation is fundamental to the path. This understanding fills me with a profound sense of joy as I see the sacred in everything around me. Communicating with nature brings me immense happiness. I recognize the Divine essence of the natural world, nurturing my soul and deepening my connection to the universe.

My goal on this journey is to become one with my True self. I am awakening to the realization that I can merge my consciousness with my higher self. When I align with this truth, life unfolds with effortless magic. My life's undeniable truths are synchronicity, serendipity, meaningful coincidences and events. They serve as a reminder of the interconnectedness of all things and the presence of inner guidance.

Training the mind to align with and serve our higher consciousness is a transformative practice on this journey. By anchoring

Anchoring the mind in the present moment is a gateway to experiencing the truth of our existence.

the mind in the present moment, we can access the truth of our existence. Cultivating present-moment awareness and inner stillness allows us to grasp the essence of "I am."

The concept of Oneness holds a special place in my heart. It symbolizes an intricate, interconnected web of energy and consciousness that unites all living beings and elements of existence. This radiant network is deeply intertwined with the Divine, and whenever I reflect upon it, I feel a sense of inner peace enveloping me. Collective consciousness is evolving towards greater awareness and comprehension. The resurgence of elevated consciousness is fundamental to my mission here on Earth.

"My Journey of Joy" is an ever-evolving journey that guides me toward a deeper understanding of myself and the world around me. It is a continuous exploration of inner joy and alignment with a higher purpose. As I navigate this path, I remain committed to embracing the beauty of life, cultivating gratitude, and quietly and humbly spreading love and light to all I encounter.

A wise one said:

Be still and breathe, ever patiently. The web of life has woven what is to be, but you must still choose your path. In time, you will see that when you listen to the wise one that dwells within, you will walk the path in balance and be free.

Author Unknown

Act from your Highest Vision

Always act from your highest vision. Then, your vision grows. This is my highest vision right now: On the path of joy, I accept and love others for who they are as they are. I don't try to change or force anyone. I allow people to be who they are. I allow myself to be who I am. I judge no one. I make choices that bring me joy. I allow things to be what they are.

The power lies within my being. My presence alone brings change. Over the years, I've learned that either the person changes or they leave. I don't have to do anything but be myself. Setting aside my agendas, I allow my joy compass to guide me. When I see an opportunity to uplift things, I do. I speak my truth. I am here to bring the tone, the tone of life, the vibration of the presence of the divine. The vibration does the orchestration at the invisible level of creation. Serendipity and synchronicity appear in unexpected places like magic, without any apparent effort.

I let go of fixing or changing people. This internal work is challenging for me. I'm still in the change process. I have always been an agent of change. My training was: if you see it, it is yours to do; if you see a hole, you fill it. Rather than criticize and complain, you do something to right it. That was my vision during my adult years, from age 29 to 66. My old framework was: I can see a problem. I can see ways for change. I can make it flow better or be more efficient. I improve it. I make it more focused and more fun. I saw it as my responsibility. I was as busy as a beaver. It was who I was for the first sixty-six years of my life. It was a great life. I loved it. I was driven. I never said, "No".

When I was sixty-six years old, my daughter Bonnie passed from this earth. I could no longer use that old mode of operation. I had no fortitude to push through or make it manifest. Another way emerged, the way of being, revealed to me moment by moment as I lived love and joy—no more focus on doing. Now, I don't have to do everything. When I see a "problem," I change my thinking. I see an "opportunity" to connect with my heart and offer love. I trust that by loving and lifting it up to the Divine to transmute, the problem will transform. It does.

Now, I am taking care of myself and doing only what is mine to do.

In retirement, it's a better way for me to live. I prefer the ease of a more natural, balanced life. I no longer carry the weight of the world on my shoulders. Like the eagle with perspective, I see from a place of wisdom.

How to Use This Book

Welcome to your Journey to Joy. This book is a transformative guide to joy and personal growth. Here is how to best use it.

Sequential Journey: Be all-in! Follow the 52-week structure sequentially, just as I did. Allow yourself to be fully immersed in the step-by-step process of transformation. Be sure to complete the weekly journal prompts. Go at your own pace. Give yourself as much time as you need. You're invited to express your heart through any form of art media.

Resource or Reference: This book covers a wide range of topics related to joy, from calming the nervous system to embracing personal boundaries. If a particular topic or theme resonates with you, feel free to navigate directly to those sections in the table of contents. Dive deeper into the insights that call to you.

Intuitive Reading: Open the book with an open heart and let the page fall open and speak to you in the moment. Trust your intuition to guide you to the wisdom you need.

Personal Journal: Use this book as inspiration to create your own personalized "Joy Journal." Document your experiences, reflections and evolution of your journey.

Experiential Practices: Engage in the various exercises and activities suggested, such as the five keys sections, breathing exercises, meditations, visualizations, and ways to cultivate gratitude, personal responsibility, and connection with nature. Experiment with these and integrate them into your daily life.

PART 1

FINDING JOY

Your living is determined not so much by what life brings to you as by the attitude you bring to life; not so much by what happens to you as by the way your mind looks at what happens.

—Khalil Gibran

"Joy is not in things; it is in us."

—Richard Wagner

Threads of Joy

Joy is the vibrant thread weaving through our living, guiding us towards happiness. True joy lies in the harmony between the body, mind and heart. Following passions and values brings joy. Joy permeates every aspect of our lives when we are fully present.

What are we doing in this journey of joy, and how does it benefit us? In this joy journey, as you journey with me, we explore life's workings and seek inspiration from our inner guidance. Imagine the light reflected by disco globe mirrors representing each aspect of the path to joy. As we ponder and contemplate these facets, we share the insights and wisdom gained from our experiences. This process deepens our understanding of joy and fosters continuous learning and personal growth. This transformative journey empowers us to shape and influence our world. Join me on this journey of self-discovery, where we can discover joy in the little things and shine our light on those around us. Together, we can create a ripple effect of happiness and make a meaningful difference.

Open to Blessings: Conversations with the Beach Warrior

As John and I walked along the beach one morning, an unusual sight caught our eyes. A big white middle-class man, who we later found out was a US veteran from Texas, was focused intently on the beach with a litter picker, one of those claw-like tools. He appeared happy and content with his task of grabbing beach litter.

Intrigued by the activity, John struck up a conversation with him. John asked him about his purpose, and he shared his routine with us. Wherever he is, he combs the beaches, picking litter. It is his way of doing his part in cleaning up the earth. When he travels, he brings three picker-uppers, aptly named "Grabber Reacher tool" to aid him in this endeavor.

Listening to his story, I couldn't help but be inspired. He explained that no matter where he finds himself, the beaches are always pristine because of his efforts. Instead of soaking up the sun and indulging in leisurely activities, he takes action. He said, "It keeps my mind engaged."

By dedicating himself to this task, he feels satisfied. It has become his way of contributing to the betterment of his world. In his eyes, each small environmental stewardship impacts him wherever he is. This encounter with the man on the beach fills me with hope. This sign of hope serves as a reminder that positive change is possible. It reassures me that the world is gradually transforming positively because of people like this man.

The Creative Conversation

Welcome to a Creative Conversation where mutual respect is the core attitude. In this conversation, we encourage participants to contribute as they feel inspired. We have a natural sense of when it's our turn to speak, and we honor each other's input by giving everyone equal time to express their ideas. We focus on speaking from the heart, sharing our perspectives in the first person. We approach the conversation with open minds, actively listening and seeking to understand each other. Here's a simple way to remember conversation etiquette: Follow the rules of the road: stay in your lane; don't cut people off. Look both ways when changing the topic, pay attention to the signs and lights, and don't hog the conversation.

For the past forty years, my interest in creative conversation has grown as I have witnessed the emergence of joy through this form of communication. Creative conversation involves active listening, presence, and the connection of ideas. During these conversations, unexpected and unforeseen ideas arise, bringing joy and inspiration. I have personally experienced the power of creative conversation in my home and classroom, where I have encouraged open minds and active listening.

Over the years, I've felt frustrated by how many people lack the skill to engage in a creative discussion. People often dominate conversations, interrupt, go off-topic, and focus more on speaking than listening. Seeing the lack of genuine listening skills in our society is disheartening. However, I've learned to be patient and present while also easing up on the intensity of my focus. My focused listening often encourages others to open up and share their thoughts. I have learned that if I don't want to have a deep connection and know their thoughts, I need to lighten up all my listening.

My husband John and I have had the privilege of participating in creative conversations with individuals who have mastered this art over forty years; we engage in a weekly Safe Peace Conversation and Long Breathing Conversation every fortnight. These gatherings nourish our souls and provide us with a deep sense of joy and connection.

For the past eleven years, John and I have been part of a monthly "Conversation Dinner" with nine other individuals. The hosts provide the food and topic, while the guests bring the beverages. The topic is revealed at the dinner table as we begin eating, creating a sense of anticipation and curiosity. This experience is beautiful as each person contributes their ideas and insights as they are inspired. We honor and value each person's input, ensuring everyone has equal time to express themselves. Our conversations weave together like a tapestry, with one idea leading to another. We allow moments of silence, which are well-received and respected. There are no monologues, no judgments, and no goals or agendas.

In conclusion, creative conversation is about listening and sharing, where each voice is valued and respected. Throughout my journey, I've come to realize how these conversations can be transformative, as we enrich each other's lives. I will continue to nurture this art, know that sharing our thoughts lead to understanding and creativity, and appreciating the joy that comes from connecting with one another.

Week 1: Joyful Moments

"There is a voice inside of you. That whispers all day long,
"I feel that this is right for me. I know that this is wrong."
No teacher, preacher, parent, friend, or wise man can
decide. What's right for you. Just listen to the voice that
speaks inside."

— Shel Silverstein

Guidance: Look up! Focus on what's right rather than on what's wrong.

You go in the direction of your focus. Think of Light when something "wrong" is drawn to your attention. Drop into your heart and radiate love and light to that "wrong." That is how "wrong" gets transmuted. Witness to the Light. See the Light in everything. You are here to observe everything. See

> *Witness the Light.*
> *See the Light in everything.*

it, bless it, honor it, thank it, and love it. Where acknowledgment of remorse or sadness exists, forgive and love it. Thank it for the energy it has held. Release the power and give it back to pure light and love. You have it all within you. Crack out of the shell. You don't need an intermediary. Your beloved teacher is within. Just have fun and enjoy living. You are so lucky to be alive!

Realization: There is no place that the light is not.

Light is what I am. Light is with me. Light is in me and all around me everywhere. I forgive all people who have hurt or harmed me. I ask forgiveness for hurting or harming anyone. I am sorry. The people I have hurt are now open to an opportunity to forgive. If they can't, it is their choice. I forgive them. Forgive and forget. Move forward. Look up. Focus on the Light. I am just listening to myself. The truth is in each one of us, waiting to be uncovered.

Knowing I am here to love and experience the joy of living gives me the freedom to be happy amidst the chaos in the world. Grief will come through deaths and disasters. It is not mine to cross the invisible line that drops me into the abyss of sorrow. The invisible line is like the electric fence for dogs to keep them from wandering off. When I touch that invisible boundary, I get the zap, "My Grief Boundary!" I know what it is. Stay away, that's not for me. I have done grief work for many lifetimes. It is no longer mine to do. I am here to love and experience the joy of living. Being me, seeing the truth. Having an honest, reflective, insightful conversation and talking with my children and grandchildren brings me great joy.

5 Keys to Being Joyful

1. Gratitude.

2. Mindfulness.

3. Know we are here to love and experience the joy of living.

4. The freedom to be happy amidst the chaos in the world.

5. A joy mindset is a choice.

Joyful Moments

- Walking pain-free after four previous days of hip pain.

- Writing a thank you note to a friend.

- Providing my perspective to a friend.

- Receiving a phone call and having a light conversation with my daughter.

- Asking a person to change something and finding they were pleased to comply.
- Interacting with a competent, helpful, and pleasant Wi-Fi tech guy.
- Watching the sunset.

Journal

What joyful moments did you have this week? Reflect quietly for a few moments and then answer the question.

Joyful Moments: Reflect and freely write from your heart about your weekly joy experience and/or any insights you may have. Express your heart through art.

Week 2: Kindness

"Kindness is a language, which the deaf can hear and the blind can see."

—Mark Twain

Guidance: You can change a situation by changing your attitude towards it.

Be kind to yourself even when you've messed up. Everything is working to perfection, even if you don't see it. It may be one of the hardest things for you to do. Admit your fault, learn from it, see from a radiant perspective, do what you need to do, and do that next time.

You are in the process of change. Forgive yourself. It brings change. Do not accept any abuse towards you. Don't speak harmful words or think negative thoughts about yourself. Be the matador. Let it go. Stay present. Don't miss the moment that is

> *When something is not working, change it.*

happening now. Listen to your inner guidance, as it provides you with the guidance on your journey. Things will change and get better.

You are in a process. Do what's right. If doing what your "right" idea is keeping you in a downward spiral, then change your idea of what is right. You can figure that out independently—it's time to upgrade your programming. When something is not working, change it.

Surround yourself with the people you love and those who love you. Leave the sad sacks alone. If you are depressed and miserable all the time, seek professional help. Once in a while, we all feel sad, but it is not supposed to be eternal. Change your thinking. Change the way you look at things. Change the belief that is creating sadness for you. We are all entitled to

> *We are all entitled to be happy.*

be happy. It is an inside job that lasts. Let's not waste our lives on things that are not ours to do. You are so loved. Feel that in your whole body.

Realization: I always thought I was supposed to listen to people's problems and help them.

"The good person listens . . ." Since my daughter passed, I have no heart tolerance to hear from people who come to me with their same repetitive earthly woes. I can listen to "A Woe Is Me" once, maybe even a second time, but never a third time. Jesus said, "Take up your bed and walk." It goes against my whole authentic being to enable and perpetuate the "woe is me" attitude in another. I am kind when

I stop reinforcing this behavior. So, people I thought were my friends dropped like flies.

I apologize for the part I played in keeping my friends stuck in their human patterns. I no longer do that. If you encounter me doing it, please point it out. Old habits die hard. When I forget, I am kind to myself. I am all about walking my talk and being true to my highest vision.

We are going to reprogram our human consciousness for kindness. Kindness is part of one's true nature, but most have forgotten this aspect. We need a memory jolt. Want a new habit? Keep reading.

Kindness is part of one's true nature.

One practical suggestion is to "be kind." By dropping into our hearts and aligning with love, we can set ourselves up to practice kindness. This practice requires daily meditation on kindness. Still the mind, observe, and stay in the present moment. The practice of authentic kindness makes a meaningful difference in our world and the larger world. We only do what's ours to do. We choose to use discernment.

When the default to rescue or save appears, become cognizant. Listen with kindness. Is this ours to do? Listen. This is all

The practice of authentic kindness makes a meaningful difference in our world and the larger world.

part of a relearning or retraining of the programmed capacities that aren't attuned to our true nature. It doesn't happen overnight.

Patience and a desire for authentic expression of kindness will open new synaptic pathways in the brain. The more one practices, the more precise the brain pathways and natural energetic flow become. They become a well-worn hiking trail in the forest. Kindness becomes automatic with practice. It's like bike riding; we don't have to think about it. We get on and ride. Kindness fosters positive relationships.

5 Keys to Kindness

1. Be kind in the present moment.
2. Practice daily meditation on kindness.
3. Use discernment and only do what is yours to do.
4. Become cognizant and listen with kindness.
5. Cultivate patience and a desire for authentic expression of kindness.

Moments of Kindness

- My grandson taught me the instructions to the Mastermind game.
- Another grandson showed me the steps to see the patterns in the game.
- I held the door open for a stranger behind me.
- I listened to an intense traumatic story.
- My granddaughter gave up her room for a week while we stayed with her family.
- Another grandson helped lift some heavy objects for me.
- It was an act of kindness that John and I did to help my son and my six grandchildren during the school week while their mother took a holiday.

Journal

What acts of kindness did you experience this week? Reflect for a few moments and answer the question.

Joyful Moments: Reflect and freely write from your heart about your weekly joy experiences or any insights you may have. Express your heart through art.

Week 3: Blessings

"Count your blessings, not your problems."

—Unknown

Guidance: **The two keys to the Art of Living are to stay in the present moment and trust the creative process of life.**

The creative process is a way to align with the power of the universe. It unfolds naturally. In stillness, you find peace and strength amidst turmoil. Shine your light on darkness, bring ease into disease, order into chaos, and love and beauty into fear and horror. Align with the creative process and relinquish human efforts and self-centeredness. Trusting that everything is working out perfectly opens you up to receiving blessings. Avoid interfering with

Trusting that everything is working out perfectly opens you up to receiving blessings.

your ego mind and have faith in the unfolding of life. Embrace the creative process and approach it with honor and integrity. You create space for blessings to manifest by staying engaged and actively participating.

Realization: **By collectively addressing the needs of our communities and the environment, we can make our world more beautiful and harmonious.**

I am confident that there are things that come to me that I don't ask for; the Universe gives them to me. It's not good or bad; it is what it is. If anything, I assume, in some fashion, it is a blessing. I need to handle it with honor and integrity, staying in the creative process, trusting life and the process, and knowing wholeheartedly that everything is working out perfectly if I don't interfere with my ego mind.

We are here to participate in living. We do this by trusting the Creative Process and letting it work. We work with it and steward it. We are not to abort the cycle at hand. What looks like a tragedy, an overwhelming disaster, or time to blow off is an incomplete process. Don't blow off steam. Let the pressure build. Pressure is needed to move this process forward and create change. We don't look at the baby in utero and get all worked up that it's not ready to be born.

I learned about the Art of Living during my twenties and thirties by listening to Martin Exeter's weekly talks and taking Art of Living classes. However, it took practice and failure over my lifetime to understand it. Now, it all makes sense. Relax into it. Read the internal messages. Listen to inner knowing. Just as our muscles move by relaxing and contracting, so does the creative process. When we relax and contract, attuned to the natural rhythms of our life cycles, we find success, creativity, abundance, and ease. Everything shows up just when we need it. We learn what we need to know. We develop the capacities and qualities of character we need to succeed at the job. Let the creative process work and trust the natural flow of Life.

> *Let the creative process work and trust the natural flow of Life.*

I hold steady in the present moment, staying in my center, vibrational frequency, and heart. This allows me to be fully present and open to receive the blessings that come my way.

When I observe without judgment, I can discern what is mine or not. I know to leave it and avoid it if it is not mine. A wise person listens to their inner guidance. Practice observing situations and experiences without judgment. This enables you to discern what is meant for you and what is not. If something is not yours, learn to let it go and stay away from it. By tuning in and following your inner wisdom, you can align yourself with the blessings meant for you.

5 Keys to Receiving Blessings

1. Trusting life and the process.
2. Staying in the creative process.
3. Holding steady in the present moment.
4. Observing without judgment.
5. Following inner guidance.

Blessing Moments

- I felt the blessings of nature at the sea as the waves crashed the shore.

- I felt the care my spouse gave me when I was tired and needed support.

- I shared my love of motherhood and the great gift of family, children, and grandchildren with a pregnant mother who said she needed to hear the words I spoke to her.

- My daughter's enthusiasm for her new career and the blessing she will bring to her field.

- Connecting with my inner self and peace amid chaos at the airport.

- With unexpected outworking, things changed and quickly fell into place without effort, providing an unforeseen and delightful blessing.

- Making new friends in an unknown place and feeling a warm welcome and sense of home.

Journal

What brought you the feeling of blessing this week? Reflect for a few moments and answer the question.

Joyful Moments: Reflect and freely write from your heart about your weekly joy experience or any insight you may have. Let your heart express itself through art.

Week 4: Laughter

"Laughter is the best medicine that brings joy, lightness, and healing to our lives."

—Ellen DeGeneres

Guidance: Lighten up! Find the humor in being human.

Laugh at things that are just a little off, something crooked, something with a funny taste, something odd, something ridiculous, something illogical, something confusing, something too tight, something too loose. Find a chuckle in whatever presents a distraction or inconvenience, no matter how difficult it may seem. Finding humor will lighten things up.

In those moments when you feel low, embrace the power of a simple smile. Let that smile grace you and witness how it effortlessly brightens your day. Pause, glance into the mirror, and observe a smile's transformative effect on your well-being. You'll be amazed at how much better you feel, as if a weight

Find something to smile about and watch what unfolds.

has been lifted off your shoulders. In reality, you recognize that the present moment is your only moment. By fully immersing yourself in the now, you honor your past, acknowledge your future, and embrace the richness of life. So, cherish the present, which holds the key to your happiness and fulfillment. Find something to smile about and watch the laughter flow.

Realization: I am here to be with the living—not living in an imaginary world with several conversations in my head.

Reality is here in this physical realm. No place, no time, and no moment is better than the one I am in right now. Humor puts my mind in the present moment, and then I can't help but find joy in it.

Live as I am, means listening to my inner voice, focusing my mind on the present moment, and staying centered in any one of the aspects of joy. When distractions arise—like worries, regrets, and old tapes playing in the background—they can easily pull me away from the present and cause me to lose sight of who I truly am, a form of amnesia. To shake me out of it, I take a deep breath in. I take time to recenter myself by being still, paying attention to my breathing and releasing those thoughts or feelings, bringing my mind back to the now. It takes practice and gentle self-discipline to still the mind and stay present.

Authenticity emerges when I am centered in the now and observe what unfolds from a neutral position. I view challenges and distractions as opportunities for growth, blessings, and laughter. Welcoming what is and accepting challenges as they are, allow me to shift my perspective and find valuable lessons. This approach stimulates my personal growth, promotes my resilience, strengthens my inner peace, and inspires my humor.

When I am focused, my mind is fully engaged in the moment, free from thoughts about the past or future. Yes, worries about what's to come or regrets about what has happened can creep in throughout the day. Feelings of being overwhelmed can surface, especially when there's so much to do and not enough time to do it. By acknowledging these feelings and returning to the present moment, I cultivate a space of peace and clarity. In that space, I can laugh at myself.

5 Keys to Humor

1. Finding humor in the unexpected.
2. Laughing at everyday challenges.
3. Embracing challenges for personal growth and laughter.
4. Living authentically and finding humor in life's distractions.
5. Discovering valuable lessons and self-connection in every challenge.

Humorous Moments

- The fish lady's story of being tricked by a guy with a counterfeit $100 bill in the Post Office, realizing it, she was chasing after him, and getting her five $20s back.
- Realizing that drinking coffee makes me a ball of energy, bouncing all over the place; change is afoot.
- Mixing the times due to difference in time zone for the Zoom call, confusing everyone.
- A friend's wonderings about a relationship with someone 30 years younger than her.
- Hearing that I have a wicked sense of humor.
- At the dinner table, listened to one humorous one-liner that flowed into the conversation.
- Watching the birds interact at the feeder.

Journal

What made you laugh this week? Reflect and explore the question in your journal at the end of each day.

Joyful Moments: Reflect and freely write from your heart about your weekly joy experience or any insights you may have. Express your heart through art.

Week 5: Heart-to-Heart Conversation

"I learned that a long walk and calm conversation are an incredible combination if you want to build a bridge"

—Seth Godin

Guidance: By embracing active listening, presence, the connection of ideas, authenticity, and equal time and respect, individuals can experience the joy and connection that emerge from creative conversation.

It allows for the emergence of unexpected ideas, the exploration of different perspectives, and the building of new insights. It creates a safe and inclusive environment where everyone's voice is valued, fostering a deep connection and inspiration. Creative conversation can be harnessed to cultivate joy and meaningful connections in the home, classroom, or within organized gatherings.

Realization: We are fully present, listening and speaking from the heart.

The other day, I had an enlightening dialogue with my eleven-year-old granddaughter. She did most of the talking while I attentively listened. She explained to me why her best friends were "best." It boils down to this: her friends listen to her without interruption, respond to what she has said, and remain on the same thread, giving personal insights and experiences. I was delighted to discover I had so much in common with my granddaughter. She already has an awareness of heart-to-heart creative conversation.

In conversations, I am present giving my full attention to the speaker. I leave my phone off. I avoid going off topic. Attentively listening, I connect with what the speaker is saying. The key to a creative conversation is authenticity and being genuine. It is an art that I have cultivated over time. The result of a creative conversation is a collective creation that leaves me exhilarated and filled with new insights. Trust and authenticity continue to grow as I engage in this practice with

> *The key to our creative conversation is authenticity and being genuine.*

others. I highly recommend embracing the power of creative conversation for anyone seeking joy and connection.

5 Keys to Creative Conversation

1. Listening.
2. Presence.
3. Connection of Ideas.
4. Authenticity.
5. Equal Time and Respect.

Creative Conversations

- I had a conversation with a dear friend; our topic was accepting what is with love.

- A friend recently shared supportive listening tips. The steps for this process are: Validate the speaker's feelings without judgment - acknowledging and accepting their emotions shows that you value and appreciate the person; be curious, ask the speaker to tell you more, and ask them about their next steps. I have been utilizing these steps. They are helping me be free of taking on other people's problems.

- During our Safe Peace Zoom, the host brought up the topic of water, leading to an hour of sharing personal connections and short stories related to it.

- In another discussion with friends, we revisited how our adult lives have led us to find our own tribe or community.

- Reflecting on wolves and the benefits of having them in the Rocky Mountain region sparked a lively discussion.

- After watching the production 'Swing State' by the Merely Players, John and I had a heartfelt discussion of the tragedies it highlighted.

Journal

What heart-to-heart conversations did you have this week? Reflect for a few moments and answer the question in your journal at the end of each day.

Joyful Moments: Reflect and freely write from your heart about your weekly joy experience or any insights you may have. Express your heart through art.

Week 6: Satisfying Moments

"True inner satisfaction comes from the joy of being yourself, unapologetically."

—Oprah Winfrey

Guidance: "I am not what happened to me. I am what I choose to become." —Carl Jung

I am that I am. Whatever follows the words "I am" I manifest and becomes my reality. Therefore, I choose to say: I am love, energy, energetic, truthful, appreciative, fit, strong, Spirit, present, here, open, timeless, spaceless, consistent, in the world, but not of it, joyful, happy, beautiful, beauty, radiant, peaceful, on my own journey, kind, integrity, harmony, balance, serene, stillness, strength, intelligent, competent, giving, logical, rational, honest, compassion, understanding, calm, gentle, tender, authentic, vulnerable, disciplined, self-controlled, restrained, forgiving, humble, supportive , empowered, whole, healthy, wholistic, courage, brave, accurate, factual, reliable, trustworthy, trusting of the Creative Process, thankful, responsible, content, stewarding the Earth, confident, encouraging, inspirational, instinctual, intuitive, centered, unwavering, selfless, all things, free from all attachments, perseverance, persistent, ethical morality, patience, diligence, truthfulness, determination, tenacity, deeply grateful, cooperative, accepting, positive, reflective, solitude, organized, loving-kindness, equanimity, simplicity, transformative, caring, connection, boundaries, sensible, light, life, eternal, without beginning or end, sincere, aware, perfect love, capable, enough, complete, perfect, safe, protected, thriving, positive change, accessible, comfortable, Divinely guided, fulfilled, willing, belonging, closeness, receptivity, welcome, prosperity, abundance, actively listening, humor, fun, laughter, enthusiasm, home, wellness, sacred, fluid, limitless, nurturing, gratitude, playful, soft, holding, enjoyment, oneness, practical, breath, accessible, beloved, loved, and wise, flexible, focused, patient, assured, respectful, giving, attentive, courteous, polite, steadfast, a protector, firm, undeviating, bold, powerful, a guide, fiery, discerning, insightful, creative.

How do you feel when you read the above? We all have access to these beautiful qualities within us. When an excuse comes up, take a moment to look at it. See the block. Acknowledge the truth. There are no more excuses. Whatever follows, "I am" will be manifested. Love yourself first.

Realization: I am satisfied with my life, the people in it, and the distance between us.

I ask for nothing more. Whatever my wants are, I let go of them. What I have right now is perfect for me. I realize, recognize and love what is. Then, I can enjoy life. I was specially planned and prepared for who I am.

I am here to focus on the feeling of peace, the vibration of peace. I am here to be in the present moment, meeting what it brings with love and light. This work satisfies me deeply.

5 Keys to Satisfaction

1. Focus.
2. Meaningful Work.
3. Being Present.
4. Being.
5. Pursue Passions.

Satisfying Moments

- Connecting with Grandmother Tree.
- Finding non-animal foods as a solution to my gallbladder inflammation.
- Self-care: resting, reading.
- Walking everywhere.
- Practicing mindfulness.
- Watching a two-year-old boy drum enthusiastically.
- Getting a total of eight hours of uninterrupted sleep.

Journal

What satisfying moments did you have this week? Reflect and answer the question in your journal at the end of each day.

Joyful Moments: Reflect and freely write from your heart about your weekly joy experience or any insights you may have. Express your heart through art.

Week 7: Happy Moments

"Happiness is not something ready-made. It comes from your actions."

—Dalai Lama

Guidance: **You are entitled to be happy. Happiness is an inside job. You are irreplaceable.**

No other person is just like you. You have something exceptional to bring to the family of man. Your contribution is one-of-a-kind to you. You can be happy in any moment. It is your choice. When you come from a place of kindness, compassion and understanding, you see with an open heart. Even if someone is hateful you can look under their mask and see their inner light.

Realization: **Regarding the family of man, we are all interconnected.**

We share a common humanity, and within that, we find countless happy moments to celebrate. Despite our differences in culture, beliefs, and backgrounds, we are all part of the same human family. Let's recognize and celebrate the diversity within our world community. Each individual adds their unique perspective, experience, and talents to the richness of our collective human experience. By embracing this diversity, we can learn from one another, broaden our horizons, and foster a more inclusive and understanding society. At the same time, it's crucial to remember our shared humanity. We all have basic needs, desires, and emotions. We all experience joy, pain, love, and loss. Recognizing our commonalities helps us to empathize with one another and build bridges of understanding and compassion.

Let's wake up from this illusion in a world that can sometimes feel divided. We are all part of the same family. Treating each other with respect and kindness will help create a harmonious and inclusive world. Let's embrace our shared humanity and strive for a

> *Treating one another with respect and kindness will help create a harmonious and inclusive world.*

global community that values and uplifts every human family member.

Change Thinking and Feelings Change

What I find is what I am looking for. I find what I'm looking for. I look for hate, and I find hate. I look for love, and I find love. I look for sadness and I find sadness. If I look for dishonesty, I see dishonesty. I look for beauty, I find beauty, and so on and so forth.

Therefore, I need to take note of my perception. Taking note of my perception, I avoid judging what I see as good or bad. My judgment colors what I see and find. How do I know if I am judging what I see as good or bad? It is a judgment that colors what I see, what I find and the outcome of my experience. For example, I see a feather, I feel a spark of curiosity. I pick it up. I examine it. My judgment colors my experience with the feather. Suppose I see it as beautiful. Then I have an excellent interchange with it. I am grateful. I feel love. If I see the feather is ugly, dirty, germy and not good enough, I have another experience. I wouldn't say I like it. I ignore it.

Here's where "change your thinking, change your feelings" comes in. Change your thinking, and your feelings will change. Instead of judging, observe and wonder about the attributes and characteristics of the things you encounter. I change my thinking, and my feelings change.

1. I see the feather.

2. I am curious. I wonder. Without judging, I notice its attributes and characteristics: the color, the size, the shape, the texture. I wonder: Who dropped it? Where has it been? How did it get here?

3. I thank the bird, the feather, and the Creator for showing this feather to me. It is not bad or good. It is.

4. Now, I understand its gift. I feel love. Now, this process can be applied to anything, not just feathers.

The SOFT process stands for See, Observe, Feel, and Thank. It can enhance your understanding, connection, and emotional well-being.

5 Keys to Happiness

1. Look for what you want.

2. Avoid judgment.

3. Change your thinking.

4. Express gratitude.

5. Apply the SOFT process.

Happy Moments

- Watching the Scarlett Macaws feeding in their natural habitat.

- Swimming in the Caribbean Sea.

- Walking three miles without my hip hurting.

- Turning over 25 pairs of nearly new running shoes to the running club.

- Finding just the suitable wooden hand carving for my son.

- Having a wish come true: I saw a Blue Morpho butterfly in its natural habitat while walking a trail in the Mayan Jungle.

- Finding the food to eat that did not aggravate my gallbladder.

Journal

What happy moments did you have this week? Reflect and answer the question in your journal at the end of each day.

Joyful Moments: Reflect and freely write from your heart about your weekly joy experience or any insights you may have. Express your heart through art.

Week 8: "I Can" Mindset

"Energy cannot be created or destroyed; it can only be changed from one form to another."

—Albert Einstein

Guidance: You are capable of more than you will ever know.

Stop thinking limiting thoughts. Catch yourself when you think something negative about yourself and others. Old habits die hard. Keep at it. You will see a change in yourself. Remember what your mother always said, "If you don't have something nice to say, don't say it!" Nothing can stop you! Go for it!

Realization: The state of one's mind shows up in one's body.

I am taking steps to keep my body strong and flexible. I have changed my mindset from "I can't" to "I can". My mindset has changed! My consciousness has shifted. I am not buying into the negativity of aging. Keep moving! I do what it takes to keep my body strong and flexible to fully engage in doing what I love.

I love kayaking for the pleasure of it! I love being in the midst of nature, being on the water, the birds, the coves, the clouds, and even the wind! The thought of returning to kayaking brings me great joy!

I felt sad when I thought I might never kayak again because my body wasn't up to it. Then I came across Ernestine Shepherd on the Internet. She inspired me and gave me hope. I read her book and website. I knew then that if it was true for her, it was true for me. I could not give up kayaking. I had done everything I could to get my body in shape, but my body was constantly aching after anything I did.

After listening to a friend talk about her longevity class, an idea popped into my head. "I needed a physical trainer!" I went online, and the only thing I could find that suited me was Catacombs Gym. Deciding to do that, I made an appointment to consult with Suzanne. Meeting with Suzanne, I told her my desire to return to kayaking. She suggested two options that would help me get back into kayaking. I chose the physical trainer option and signed up for physical training. It was the best decision. It has given me new hope for my future endeavors as I age.

What exercises are provided by your coach to build your physical strength, trust, and confidence for kayaking? My coach, Brian Miller, at Catacombs Gym, coached me to develop my physical strength, trust, and confidence for kayaking: balance in getting in and out of the kayak, endurance for paddling, and strength for lifting and carrying my kayak.

Now, I am getting acquainted with muscles that have become inactive due to fear and a lack of confidence in my body's capabilities. I am on the path of longevity. Thanks to Brian for his encouragement and expertise in physical training, proving that my body is trustworthy.

5 Keys to "I Can" Mindset

1. Mindset shift.
2. Inspiration and motivation.
3. Seeking professional guidance.
4. Consistency and dedication.
5. Trust in the body.

Journal

How did you acquire an "I Can" mindset this week? Reflect and answer the question.

Joyful Moments: Reflect and freely write from your heart about your weekly joy experience or any insights you may have. Express your heart through art.

Week 9: Truth and Honesty

"Honesty is the first chapter in the book of wisdom."

—Thomas Jefferson

Guidance: The truth sets you free. You're here to bring the truth.

Therefore, you move along in your process. People might not like what you bring. You may lose friends. The ones who stay have substance and endure. The truth needs to be told. The truth frees and opens you to see clearly. More realizations come. You continue your expansion of consciousness.

There's an art to telling the truth without burning bridges. Stay in the vibration of love before, during, and after truth-telling. Trust in the process. Whatever comes next, be thankful. Truth brings clarity. Embrace honesty and stay true to yourself as you follow the path that aligns with your values and beliefs. Reflect on your significant life experiences, thoughts, and the emotions that changed you. Write about the underlying beliefs and values you had at that time. What did you learn? What truths were revealed to you? Are they still influencing you today?

What principles or ideals are most important to you? Identify what drives your decisions, actions, and behaviors. What underlying values show up? Here are some possibilities: honesty, integrity, compassion, freedom, respect, fairness, justice, and growth.

Question and challenge your values and beliefs. Do they align with your true self? Why do you hold particular views? Are they based on evidence or societal expectations? Do those views no longer serve you or align with your authentic self? Have you been living from a limited perspective? Be honest with yourself.

Seek different perspectives. To get a more comprehensive understanding of your values, have conversations with people who hold different beliefs. Do not try to change their thinking. Listen and see their viewpoint. What rings true? Can you expand your thinking to understand their perspective?

Align your expression. With an understanding of your values and beliefs, focus on aligning them with your living. Make choices and decisions that reflect your core values. In this way, you express your highest vision. Remember, this is an ongoing process. Your values and beliefs can evolve and change over

Your core truth determines everything you think, feel, say, and do.

time as you gain new experiences and insights. Your core truth determines everything you think, feel, say, and do. Your core truth comes with a truth yardstick you can use in decision-making. When you are not in alignment, you'll know it.

Realization: Seek and live the truth.

When I am honest, my body feels relaxed and flows with life. When I have dissonance between my heart and mind, a trigger is observed, and my body feels uncomfortable. This tells me I need to check in with myself and be honest. What value or belief was being disrespected? What beliefs and values were challenged? What boundary was crossed? I choose to get to the bottom of it and to resolve it. Stuffing it is not an option. It makes matters worse. As a result of doing this work, I relax, and my heart and mind are at peace. I feel calm, with an overall sense of well-being. By being honest, I can live with myself. Honesty is the foundation for trust. I trust myself.

Journal

Reflect on your significant life experiences, thoughts, and emotions that have changed you.

- Write about the underlying beliefs and values you had at that time.
- What did you learn?
- What truths were revealed to you?
- Are they still influencing you today?
- What principles or ideals are most important to you? Identify what drives your decisions, actions, and behaviors.
- What underlying values emerge? Some possibilities are honesty, integrity, compassion, freedom, respect, and growth.
- Question and challenge your values and beliefs.
- Do your values and beliefs align with your true self?

- Why do you hold particular views?
- Are they based on evidence or societal expectations?
- Do those views no longer serve you or align with your authentic self?
- Have you been living from a limited perspective?
- Be honest with yourself.
- Seek different perspectives.

5 Keys to Honesty

1. Question and Challenge Values and Beliefs.
2. Seek Different Perspectives.
3. Align Your Expression With Your Core Truth.
4. Reflect on Life Experiences and Values.
5. Be Honest With Yourself.

Honest Moments

- I am sensitive to joking about things that are important to me.
- I gave my honest feedback and insight to a friend.
- I apologize for the wrong I have done to others.
- Admitting I did not know the topic, I am interested and willing to learn.
- Realizing my boundaries, I kindly stated what I needed. Love is always the answer. I was heard and openly received.
- I faced the reality of my hip and made an assessment. I have a plan. I am committed to strengthening and integrating the use of my upper body for movement in kayaking and dancing.
- I overbought an item I forgot that I already owned.

Journal

What brought you honesty this week? Reflect and answer the question.

Joyful Moments: Reflect and freely write from your heart about your weekly joy experience or any insights you may have. Express your heart through art.

Week 10: Integrity

"You must never be fearful about what you are doing when it's right."

—Rosa Parks

Guidance: Integrity builds character and trust.

Eventually, it becomes first nature, one's true nature. It reveals who you are under all your programming. It is beyond belief. One will begin to know who one truly is.

In the car metaphor, the conscience is the engine, and the steering wheel is integrity. Integrity is the outer expression resulting from a solid, moral conscience. When the conscience is clear and functioning well, you steer yourself towards honesty, fairness, and ethical behavior. Upholding your integrity strengthens your conscience and clarifies the subconscious, leading to greater self-awareness, moral clarity, and emotional stability that eventually reflects in the outer world. Trust the inner engine and steer your life in the right direction.

This combination acts as the fuel that powers your engine of conscience, enabling you to make better decisions, navigate life's challenges with precision. It drives you towards fulfillment and purpose, allowing you to live authentically and harmoniously with others. In essence, it creates a solid foundation for personal growth and positive interactions with the world.

As you listen to the whispers of your conscience, it guides you towards integrity. This journey involves inner work, learning and growth, helping to break the

I must live with myself and be honest with myself. I make mistakes.

chains that bind you. Following your conscience increases conscious awareness and meaningful relationships and growing in all areas of life: business, sports, career, home life, parenting and much more. Integrity and all its attributes serve as the rebar, while conscience is the foundation upon which you build your life.

Always remember to stay true to yourself and let your conscience guide you. At some point, it becomes an instinctual response, to what is presented. It is simply being yourself. You can trust your decisions.

Realization: Principles of integrity guide how I live.

I choose to live by the principles of integrity. They keep me on my life course. I follow my highest vision and do the right thing, considering the fitness of things. How does this fit right now? Is it the right time, the right place, the right words? Act and speak from that place.

I must live with myself and be honest with myself. I make mistakes. I constantly correct my course as clarity arises. I've learned to forgive myself, learn, and move on. I right myself. I am an experiential learner. I know through experience. I now sense what to stay away from. When I live to my highest vision, my highest vision keeps increasing, as does my understanding and compassion.

Hold to integrity. Recently, I received a gift wrapped in the most unattractive wrapping paper I have ever seen. The colors clashed, the design was quite messy. It had an awful smell with flies hovering over it. Brown slime smeared its sides. I felt sick. I became shaky. I felt great sadness. At first, I didn't want the gift and had reservations about it. However, I believe there is a blessing and a lesson to be found in every situation so I decided to embrace it and see what would unfold once I unwrapped it entirely.

Here is my mystery gift: I discovered today that my dear friend is also battling something that I will leave unspoken. In response to this news, I offer a prayer of gratitude and acceptance. Despite the immense sorrow I feel, I acknowledge it and understand that it represents the pain of a mother losing her beloved child. I release this sorrow to the Divine. I asked for the well-being and support of my dear friend, myself as a mother and all those who love us.

I am unable to wrap my feelings around this situation anymore. I have done all the internal work I can possibly do. I cannot fix or rescue. I am not a firefighter. I have taken that stance. I have taken an oath to stick to it. I recognize that a gift is hidden within it, and I no longer allow myself to be consumed by sorrow. Mother Earth conveyed to me last year that my time of experiencing sorrow had ended and I trust in the truth of these words. I listen attentively and follow this guidance.

How can I be compassionate, kind and understanding without being enabling? This is difficult work for me. I choose to strike a balance between support and accountability. Otherwise, I'll fall into my old patterns, rescuing, fixing and going down the rabbit hole. The key for me is to stay conscious and awake.

Here is my tried-and-true process that works for me:

Step 1: I leave the situation without immediately trying to change it.

Step 2: I take deep breaths, allowing myself to ground and find inner peace.

Step 3: I think of the Serenity Prayer. I surrender the situation to the Divine. It is out of my control. I place my trust in the creative process.

Step 4: I connect with the current of Love and Light. I allow this energy to work within and through me.

Step 5: I detach myself from the emotional ties that lead me to a state of sadness and immobilization by shifting my thinking and perspective.

Step 6: I remain held and supported by the Divine.

Step 7: I live in a state of trust, knowing that everything will work out in its own time and in its own way.

Step 8: I view my friend as doing her sacred work on Earth. I understand it is her journey and I cannot fix or rescue her. I will only take action after consulting with my inner guidance.

Step 9: Everything is working out for my friend's highest good. I refrain from interfering with her journey. This is her sacred work, and I hold her in the Light, knowing that the energy of the Divine permeates everything, including her.

Step 10: I hold and love my mother self. If my mother self needs to grieve, I give her the space to do so. I spend time in nature, paint and do all the things that bring me joy. I choose to be with people who lift me up and love me. I am gentle with myself and practice self-care as I continue this journey. I focus on the Light.

Finding Joy and Peace in a Difficult Situation

- Embrace the gift despite its unattractive wrapping.
- Respond with gratitude and acceptance.
- Release sorrow and seek Divine support.
- Find meaning and gifts within the situation.
- Practice self-care and staying connected to the light of Truth.

5 Keys to Integrity

1. Following one's conscience.
2. Acting with honesty and fairness.

3. Self-reflection and growth.

4. Trusting oneself.

5. Living with authenticity.

Moments of Integrity

- I returned a 3-carat diamond ring I found in a gravel parking lot to the Joyful Journey office. It was returned to the owner, who was frantically looking for it

- I followed what resonated with me rather than going along with the group.

- I expressed how I felt to a person about how I was being affected by an attitude of judgment.

- I was true to myself by keeping my distance and only doing what was mine.

- I let a person figure things out for herself and solve her own problem.

- I realized that all paths eventually lead to God. I no longer need to get anyone on my path.

- I trust I am doing the right thing.

- I am happy to be myself. I am not pleasing others. By loving myself first, I have the substance to love others.

Journal

How did integrity make itself known this week? Reflect and answer the question.

Joyful Moments: Reflect and freely write from your heart about your weekly joy experience or any insights you may have. Express your heart through art.

PART 2

OPENING TO SELF

"Training your mind to be in the present moment is the number one key to making healthier choices."

—Susan Albers

Breathing Through Pain and Healing

The cracking sound of my femur dislocating from my hip joint and the pain set my head spinning due to overdoing my routine physical therapy hip exercises. I nearly passed out. I started my slow, focused, rhythmical breathing for the cadence of thirteen. Miraculously, my femur went back in place when I plopped in the chair as my physical therapist slid it under me.

Riding in the ambulance, I was present with slow breathing as the EMT asked me questions. (When a crisis arises, life requires me to be present.) I had a pleasurable experience. He was the age of my Light daughter, Bonnie. Just thinking of her brought her presence in. So Bonnie was with me, too. The EMT was a kind young man, as were all the other first responders in the ambulance with me.

Spending the day in an emergency room, slow breathing brought me peace. I didn't feel any fear. I had a sense of well-being that all was well. I met many friendly, pleasant, caring young people: the attending nurse, the X-ray technicians, the doctor, and the physical therapist. I had a lovely time. What could have ended in surgery ended with only traumatized tissue!

The next day, I flew to Santa Rosa with my friend. We were going to a Grandmothers Net of Light Gathering. First, we visited the Redwood Forest. Using only a cane, slow breathing, and a slow pace, I walked the trail in the forest.

My hip reset itself. I attribute this outcome to slow, focused breathing. My body improved every day. Today, I have no hip problem. I am pain-free as I climb the stairs.

Week 11: Presence

"Presence is not an act, but a state of being fully engaged in the here and now."

—Oprah Winfrey

Guidance: Being Mindful in Everyday Life.

"Being" involves being present in the present moment with your heart, body, and mind aligned. It is a state of awareness and engagement with your experience at hand. When you are in a state of being, your mind is not ruminating on the past or worrying about the future but is fully immersed in the present. In presence you observe your feelings, understand the truth of your emotions, and receive insight, inspiration, and wisdom.

Your mind can be like an untrained dog that needs direction, attention, and kind discipline. Just as you would use positive reinforcement to train a dog, you can apply those same principles to train your wandering mind. When your thoughts sidetrack, gently redirect your focus, just as you would guide a dog back on track with a calm, encouraging voice. Speak to your mind with understanding and love, not harsh criticism. Tell your mind, "I see you want to chase that thought, but right now, I need you to stay present with me. Good job!" Just as you reward a dog for the desired behavior, praise your mind when it returns to the present moment. It may take repetition and patience, but over time, your mind will learn to stay focused, just as a dog learns to heel on command. With consistent, positive reinforcement, your mind will become more disciplined, allowing you to maintain presence and awareness, even amidst life's distractions.

The more you practice being in the present moment, the more

natural and effortless it will become. Your ability to stay grounded and centered will grow, and you will find that you can access a deeper sense of peace, clarity, and joy.

Realization: "Doing" can be seen as senseless unless aligned with the present moment.

When I am actively engaged in the present moment, my actions become imbued with purpose and intention. When my actions are disconnected from the present moment, they may seem empty, anxious, and meaningless. They may even be dangerous. Accidents happen when I am not fully present and engaged: car crashes, falling off ladders, crossing in traffic, slipping on the ice. I am familiar with how accidents happen. Another detriment to "spacing out" is that it negatively affects the quality of my work, leading to poor outcomes or products. Being fully present and "all-in" improves my performance in everything I do.

Often, I find myself engaging in activities automatically while my mind wanders off. True "thinking" is not a collection of separate thoughts. When my thoughts align with the present moment, my focus remains undistracted. I recognize passing thoughts as "passing clouds," transient and fleeting. Thinking brings forth the truth in the moment, which is focused, coherent, and meaningful. When my mind is in sync with my state of being, my thoughts naturally

> *When our thoughts align with the present moment, our focus remains undistracted.*

flow from a place of clarity and insight. On the other hand, when my thoughts detach from the present moment, they can lead to confusion, stress, and a sense of disconnection from myself. Another way to put it: I have unplugged from the Source of my being, which resides in the eternal present moment.

Consider washing the dishes as a multisensory, mindful experience of being, doing, and thinking. My being is present. My mind focuses on the task. My body feels and senses. My heart is feeling happy. When I wash the dishes, I am mindful of the water, temperature, the flow of water over my hands, and the dishes. I pay attention to the dish's texture, smoothness or roughness, and the scent of the soap. I am aware of the motion of my fingers, hands, and arms, as well as the posture of my body. My thoughts go to the completeness of the task, the sight of the clean dishes, and the knowing of satisfaction with a job well done.

Like the example of the mindful act of washing the dishes, I can apply mindfulness to anything I do, hear, and speak. When I am in mindfulness, I am a conduit for my being. Being, doing, and thinking function when aligned with each other and the present moment. I feel the joy of the moment. My actions and thoughts gain depth, purpose, and meaning when fully present and engaged in the now.

The greatest gift I can give is my presence. In a world filled with distractions created by the pressure of doing, the speed of production, the electronic barrage, and the anxiety of being overwhelmed, my presence is the greatest gift I can offer.

With the alignment of my still mind, open heart, and body in the present moment, I discover my true essence: one with Source. I am one with Source. There is no separation. The present moment creates a presence that can be felt and recognized. It exists in the Now. The mind can recognize it but cannot comprehend it. The mind must be still for presence to be known. Presence is a channel through which Life moves providing clarity and wisdom.

My presence is my inner home, my sanctuary. To understand this space, I must consciously connect with my presence. I receive spiritual substance through this presence, creating a deeper connection with the sacred. Love plays a

> *We co-create our New Earth, built upon love and truth, by embodying love and living to our highest vision.*

significant role in this process. It is a powerful generator of the spiritual substance for my inner home.

These concepts may appear simple. However, they require deep familiarity and experience. To understand and appreciate spiritual substance, one must actively live and engage with it. It is a love relationship. The more I know my presence, the easier it is for me to access it. Eventually, I become one. I know my presence is I am. Residing here is "love work" that is being done in momentary living. Otherwise, it remains a distant concept that is beyond reach.

Living in a state of presence, I tap into the essence from which my outer world is born. In this state, I experience deep inner peace. Through my connection with my inner home, I witness things lining up now and can accurately guess a future outcome. I have what I need when I need it. I experience synchronicity.

As I am present in each moment, I consciously cultivate love, truth, and authenticity. By being one with presence, I not only impact my capacities but also the world around me. Wherever I am, even without saying a word, I bring this power of presence. My presence is felt in the outer world. What a fun adventure this joy journey of self-discovery and transformation is! New possibilities are made known through Presence. A new world filled with love, compassion, and harmony becomes the reality. Knowing presence is the greatest gift one will ever receive.

5 Keys to Knowing Your Presence

1. Alignment of Mind, Heart, and Body.

2. Stillness of Mind.

3. Connection with Inner Home.

4. Love Relationship.

5. Co-Creation and Impact.

Moments of Presence

- Fully immersed in nature, I walked along the Florida River. I saw a Red-Tailed Hawk, a muskrat, and a robin.

- In writing in my journal, the words freely flowed. I received guidance and understanding.

- I ate breakfast being aware of all my senses as well as the people and elements who participated in the process of providing it.

- I had a deep conversation about the truth of aging.

- At the gym, I got out of my head. I felt the magic of "I can!" As I engaged in my exercises, I became aware of my breath, my muscles, and the sensations in my body.

- I had an opportunity to listen to Tara's talk and meditation on two wings of awareness: clarity and wisdom.

- As a hospice volunteer, I knew my presence when I spent time with a hospice patient. I was willing to be with him and provide what was needed. Everything flowed. We made an excellent connection.

Journal

How did you experience your presence this week? Reflect and answer the question.

Joyful Moments: Reflect and freely write from your heart about your weekly joy experience or any insights you may have. Express your heart through art.

Week 12: Finding Balance

"Self-balance is the key to a harmonious life."

—Albert Einstein

As I reflect on recent conversations with John regarding patriarchy and matriarchy, I have realized that finding self-balance is essential to transcend these systems. It is not about fixing one system or the other but about discovering and nurturing our inner equilibrium while we are connected to these systems. Just as

> *Kick and scream—it doesn't matter. Change is inevitable.*

we are, these systems are in their process of evolution, moving toward balance. Kick and scream—it doesn't matter. Change is inevitable.

Guidance: Self-balance begins by recognizing your individual approach.

You have a journey and purpose, which is crucial to honor and embrace. By acknowledging and accepting your individuality, you can align yourself with your path toward balance. As you know yourself, you feel what brings you into balance and what does not.

Understand that balance often involves interacting with individuals at different levels of consciousness. This can be tricky and requires practice. Look for what you agree on. Find the common ground and connect there. When you connect with what you agree upon, you find the starting point for dialogue. See how that feels. You may notice an overall good feeling. When you engage with those who are aware of their purpose, whether in sports, theater, community work, business, or any kind of team collaboration you will experience the power of harmony.

In your world, you coexist as couples and mixed groups, embodying a full spectrum of energies. You are not functioning separately from one another. By recognizing and honoring the contributions of all genders, you can create a harmonious society. Achieving balance requires a collective effort from everyone.

Realization: As each one of us comes into balance, the world comes into balance.

As each of us finds balance, the world will follow suit. I have the potential to make a powerful positive impact. Traditionally, at the center of family units, as a mother and grandmother, I play a significant role in achieving balance in society. I can positively influence those around me.

John also plays a crucial role in achieving balance for our family. He provides emotional stability, logical decision-making, physical strength and diverse perspectives.

The roles of the family unit are not set in stone. John and I have found a balance and work together as a cohesive unit. Roles are fluid. Sometimes, he leads while I follow and vice versa. We share input and collaborate as a team.

In our world, we coexist together embodying a full spectrum of energies. By recognizing and honoring our contributions. We can live a balanced and harmonious life. If everyone came into balance our world would reflect it.

Five Keys to Balance

1. Self-Awareness.
2. Community Engagement.
3. Flexibility in Roles.
4. Emotional Intelligence.
5. Collective Effort.

Moments of Balance

- I paced myself during Longevity gym class.

- After a three-week break from our book study, I enjoyed being with my Zoom book study friends.

- I transplanted my tomatoes in pots into the outside garden bed. After a few days of shock, they looked solid and vibrant.

- I went to my volunteer meeting, but what I planned and prepared for did not happen. Instead, an old friend showed up with his rock collection, so we did that instead of my plan. I loved his ancient rock artifacts.

- Today, I participated in the launch party podcast for the new book *Good to the Last Drop* by Irene Weinberg, in which I wrote a chapter, My Path to Joy. It became available for purchase on Amazon on June 14, 2024.

- I shared my story of making friends with Grief.

- I needed help getting the printer connected to Wi-Fi. I was unsuccessful, and I felt frustrated.

Journal

How do you cultivate balance for a lasting impact? How do you think it can benefit you? Reflect and answer the questions.

Joyful Moments: Reflect and write freely from your heart about your weekly joy experience or any insights you may have. Let your heart express itself through your art.

Week 13: Conscious Breathing

"Breathe in deeply to bring your mind home to your body"

—Thich Nhat Hanh

Guidance: The more chaotic the outer world becomes, the more you need to access your inner peace.

You could even see it as putting peace into your Inner Peace bank account. You will be able to access it and draw it forth in future times of crisis when you may not know what to do or are feeling confused about something you have never faced before. This peace will keep you calm. You will be able to think straight.

For a happy life where you are fully functioning, you need to breathe deep into your trunk (gut). This deep breath allows the breath to spiral around your back and through your stomach vertically, and the energy can flow unhindered, the whole system flowing and vibrating. Now, move to your solar plexus and do the same thing.

Feel who you are and who you came to be. Your breath makes you whole.

Repeat breathing in your heart. Then go to your brain. Feel it in your whole being. Feel who you are and who you came to be. Your breath makes you whole.

Express from your place of being. Keep your spine straight. The spine is the complete channel through which comes the Universe's focused healing and intelligence. Organs work together as a team. Your breath is the conduit. It ignites every system—circulatory, digestive, respiratory, endocrine, excretory, and nervous—every organ, every muscle, every bone, every tissue, down to DNA in every cell in your body.

All the answers to the Universe are within you. Be your guru. Go within, breathe in, and breathe out. Be conscious of the breath. In the breath, there is no fear. Fear takes you out of the reality of oneness with the Universe. Body, mind, and spirit are designed to work in sync. The breath informs the heart, the gut, and the mind. When the breath is shallow and fast, you create that existence. When it is slow and deep, then you make another existence.

Become conscious of your breath—in and out! Trust that life brings just what is needed in the moment. Listen to your heartbeat. Be present. Relax. Breathe. Do your breathing. Watch your breathing. All is well. You only know ease. It is as effortless as the breath in breathing. There is no more effort. There is no more stress. What gets done happens seemingly without effort.

Realization: I have accessed this inner peace bank account countless times.

I just was not aware of it. I thought it was because I was resilient, grounded, or my genetics. No, it is none of the former. All of it was a result of inner peace. I am internally strong because I remain centered. Take, for example, the Wi-Fi connection for my printer. I knew what to do because of the earlier substance of inner peace I both consciously and unconsciously generated. This peace was readily available in my peace bank. It calmed my mind. I knew the truth. I knew all would work out.

Keep generating peace. In crisis, it is more valuable than money. Doesn't it make sense that the Inner Peace bank account is available to everyone regardless of identity and condition? The secret is generating inner peace, letting it build, and not releasing the pressure valve. In this way, I build the substance of peace in my inner peace bank account.

Long Breathing

Although I have practiced slow breathing for many years to aid me in bringing my emotions under control, I acknowledge and thank Jonathan Macintyre for teaching me Long Breathing. Jonathan discovered Long Breathing through his intuition.

Long Breathing brought me to a whole new level of cadence, relaxation, and breathing rhythm, which I applied to my conscious breathing during my hip event. We spent seven minutes on each cadence with four different cadences. Deep peace it is!

Instruction in Conscious Breathing

Pay attention to your breath. Be aware of how you are breathing. Notice how your breathing settles when you become conscious of it. Let's start with the cadence of seven. Do this breathing pattern seven times: Breathe into a slow count of seven. Use it as you need it. Allow. No forcing or pushing. If seven is too much, cut it to four. Do the breathing count so it is comfortable for you. Decrease it to a count of four and build from there, adding as your capacity to breathe gets stronger.

See and notice how you feel. I always feel present in my body, at ease, and free of anxiety. It brings me into balance and calmness in the present moment. I suggest starting to practice Conscious Breathing now. Do it twice a day to help you get comfortable with it. Go deeply into inner peace. You'll like this! Remain there as you move through your day. When you leave that deep inner peace, return to it through the breath.

Ha Breathing

Ha or Huna breathing is a spiritual tradition from Hawaii. It helps to slow your heart rate, helping you to relax and become calm when you're feeling anxious or overwhelmed.

To start, state your intention (it must be aligned for the highest good). Align your body, mind, and heart with your intention. Do Ha Breathing: Do this pattern seven times: Breathe in to count to 7. Hold for a count of 7. Release for a count of 7. Pause and relax for a count of 7. All is well. Fear not!

What do you feel after Ha Breathing? See and notice how you feel. I always feel present in my body, at ease, and free of anxiety. It brings me into balance and calmness in the present moment. I use it when moving and releasing an old stuck pattern.

Do the breathing count so it is comfortable for you. Decrease it to a count of four and build from there, adding as your capacity to breathe gets stronger. I suggest you start practicing Ha Breathing now. To get comfortable with it, do it twice a day. To make it more of a ritual and keep my focus and count, I set out seven small stones and move one stone as I complete each breath. Then, I save the stones to use later.

5 Keys to Conscious Breathing

1. Slow breathing can help with pain management and relaxation.
2. Long Breathing is a technique that takes slow breathing to a new level.
3. Conscious breathing can be practiced using a simple pattern.
4. Ha Breathing is another technique that can be beneficial.
5. Being conscious of the breath and practicing slow breathing can lead to a peaceful life.

Journal

What role does conscious breathing play in your own life? How do you think it benefits you? Reflect and answer the questions.

Joyful Moments: Reflect and write freely from your heart about your weekly joy experience or any insights you may have. Let your heart express itself through your art.

Week 14: Inner Silence

"Silence is the language of God; all else is poor translation."

—Rumi

***Guidance:* Feel the power of your breath; inhale the breath of life.**

Take a deep breath through your nose, feel it filling your chest, expanding your belly, flowing through your legs, and reaching your toes. Breathe freely and deeply, allowing the breath to reach every cell of your body. Slowly exhale through your mouth, letting your breath lead the way. Keep repeating this process, embracing inner silence with each breath.

***Realization:* During my Long Breathing session today, I felt a deep connection to something greater than myself—an experience that transcends explanation.**

In truth, the most fitting description is inner silence. In this space, thoughts, emotions, and distractions fade, allowing for complete awareness of the present moment. I experienced oneness with everything accompanied by a deep calm, joy and peace.

Deep breathing, mindful meditation, and immersing myself in nature are the most effective ways to access inner silence. Requires no financial investment or specialized tools.

A Dialogue between John and me: Weaving the previous weeks' threads of presence, balance, and breathing, John and I consider inner silence and its vital role in creating an inner sanctuary space, ultimately connected to the joy experience.

Anita: I knew the profound sense of presence, a connection to something greater than myself today during Long Breathing. It is both inexplicable and indescribable. Something one needs to experience to understand. It is a state of being where thoughts, emotions, and external distractions fade away. It allows for inner awareness and connection to the present moment. I felt at one with all that is, a deep sense of calm, joy, and peace. Deep breathing, mindful meditation, and being with nature

> *Inner silence! Everything shifts when we embrace that moment of silence.*

are some ways I experience inner silence. I highly recommend it. It doesn't cost money or require tools. Breathe, breathe in the breath of life. Breathe deep through your nose, into your chest, into your belly, down through your legs, into your toes. Allow the breath to go where it wants into every cell of your body. Then, using your mouth, exhale slowly. Let your breath guide the process. Now, repeat this process again and again. Inner silence! Everything shifts when we embrace that moment of silence. We know now when to be quiet and allow silence to create a sacred space. We can tap into our spiritual essence within this holy space. Together, we amplify the sanctuary space.

John: A one-liner that comes to me is, "Be still and know who I am." Those are some serious words. I mean, think about your being in a group. And there's silence, right? You let that silence be "Be still" there. And feel how that feels. Be in that, and it's like the ether. The ether of silence is where God is. It's where God can be realized. You can absorb it. You can perceive God more easily in that space.

5 Keys to Inner Silence

1. Be present: When fully present in the moment, you experience the power of silence. It requires letting go of distractions and immersing yourself in the present moment.

2. Cultivate a sacred space: By caring for, nurturing, and tending your inner garden, you can deepen your connection with the Divine.

3. Love generates spiritual substance: Approaching silence and sacred space with love amplifies our transformative potential and ability to perceive and know the Divine.

4. Embrace ease and lightness: Remember, "The yoke is easy, and my burden is light." Co-creating is never a burden; otherwise, you are not co-creating with the Divine. Being in oneness brings a sense of ease and lightness.

5. Be one with the vibration of silence: To truly comprehend and integrate the power of silence, immerse yourself in it. It goes beyond mere conceptual knowledge. It's like trying to teach calculus to a first grader. You must live, experience, and allow it to become a part of your being.

Joy Moments of Inner Silence

- I experienced inner silence during my breathing practice.

- I experienced inner silence during group meditation.

- I experienced inner silence during Sunday's Safe Peace Zoom.

- I experienced inner silence while watching the finches at the bird feeder.

- I experienced inner silence while amending the garden soil.

- I experienced inner silence during my morning stretching practice.

- I experienced inner silence while walking in nature.

Journal

How do you work with inner silence in your life? How does it benefit you? Reflect and answer the questions.

Joyful Moments: Reflect and write freely from your heart about your weekly joy experience or any insights you may have. Let your heart express itself through your art.

Week 15: Inner Peace

"Peace comes from within. Do not seek it without."

—Buddha

Guidance: Peace is the feeling of lightness in your body.

It is a flow of energy, a vibration, and a frequency that brings you to your inner happy home. It brings relaxation, clarity, flow, presence, freedom, and liberation. In other words, it's your personal peace and harmony meter, telling you that you're in sync with yourself.

The sensations of inner peace as a vibrational flow of energy can vary from person to person but commonly include Warmth and Lightness, Tingling Sensation, Emotional Release, Clarity and Focus, Connection and Oneness and Deep Relaxation.

Inner peace is the freedom to rest in the assurance that everything works for the highest good. All is well. The sensations of inner peace, as a vibrational flow of energy, can be calming, uplifting, and spiritually enriching.

> *Inner peace is the freedom to rest in the assurance that everything works for the highest good.*

Realization: No matter what life presents, I can hold my inner peace where the external forces of the world do not control my heart, mind, and body.

I remain in alignment with the truth of myself. I can choose to hear my heart, my mind, and my body's messages. Ultimately, I can listen and choose my expression from inner peace. Knowing this truth is the path to true freedom.

5 Keys to Inner Peace

1. Connect with Your Inner Happy Home.
2. Embrace the Sensations of Inner Peace.
3. Rest in the Assurance of Divine Order.
4. Remain Aligned with Your Truth.
5. Find True Freedom in Inner Peace.

Moments of Inner Peace

- Mindful meditation and breathing.
- Relaxing in a hot bath with lavender and Epsom salts.
- Playing the singing bowl.
- Working in the garden soil.
- Walking in nature among the Juniper trees.
- Morning yoga practice.
- Journal writing.

Journal

When did you experience inner peace this week? How does it benefit you? Reflect and answer the questions.

Joyful Moments: Reflect and write freely from your heart about your weekly joy experience or any insights you may have. Let your heart express itself through your art.

Week 16: Serenity

"Serenity is not the absence of chaos but the presence of serenity within oneself."

—Albert Einstein

***Guidance:* Serenity is a state of peacefulness, calmness, tranquility, and inner peace free from stress, anxiety, or disturbance.**

When someone experiences serenity, they often feel harmony and contentment. By embodying a calm presence, you can cultivate peace and tranquility. Instead of engaging with someone unhinged and ranting, you can embody peace, calmness and serenity. With compassion and understanding, you can hold space for sorrow and fear and bounce back from chaos without judgment, maintaining your serenity.

Serenity is always present within. You spend too much time in your head. Breathe. Drop into your heart. Connect with the still point. Breathe. Observe. Now, you are in your inner garden. Now, you can be with whatever comes to you.

Taking care of ourselves is crucial for the success of our mission. Self-care may be seen as selfishness, but it is not.

Your path in life reveals your mission, and your inner stillness allows your inner compass to function, guiding you towards serenity. You are on a mission, and it is up to you to fulfill it.

Realization: **Taking care of myself is crucial for the success of my mission.**

Self-care may be seen as selfishness, but it is not. I must love myself and do this by self-care. If I don't love myself, I can't give my whole self to others. I choose to nurture and treat myself with the same love and care a loving, balanced mother gives. Eat right, exercise, and care for my body. I focus on peace and serenity, watering my consciousness's seeds of peace and love. Knowing serenity comes with consistent still point practice.

5 Keys to Serenity

1. Align with the feeling of a calm presence.
2. Hold space with compassion and understanding.
3. Connect with inner stillness.
4. Follow your life's mission.
5. Practice self-care.

Moments of Serenity

- Watching a breathtaking sunrise.
- Watching the awe-inspiring sunset.
- Gazing at a star-filled night sky.
- Sitting by an icy pond.
- Walking through my quiet neighborhood.
- Feeling the still place within myself.
- Watching the deer munching on grass.

Journal

What brought you the feeling of serenity this week? How did it benefit you? Reflect and answer the questions.

Joyful Moments: Reflect and write freely from your heart about your weekly joy experience or any insights you may have.

PART 3

FINDING HOME

The ache for home lives in all of us, the safe place where we can go as we are and not be questioned.

—Maya Angelou

Home in Vibration

The most powerful experience I can have with myself is vibrational. I bring love to consciousness and feel that energy. Chemistry, magic, the feeling of love, reverence, sacredness and inner peace, it's indescribable. It is my home. It's just being able to stay with that vibration that allows me to hear the tone of my creator. Something happens when people are physically together, but there's something even more potent when you connect vibrationally. Silence is a powerful tool for communicating at a vibrational level with one another. You know it, when you feel it, everyone is vibrationally humming with that tone. When two are in agreement and a third tone sounds, it creates a unified radiation of energy. When I bring this tone to consciousness, my silence has more vibrational impact on the people I am with, than the words I say. Unspoken but understood.

— John Albright Sr.

Close Encounter with Nature

The other day, my friends and I observed an exciting encounter with nature on the Halifax River. Before I can tell you that story, I must tell you about the beautiful Halifax.

The Halifax is a river that flows twenty-five miles south along the intracoastal waterway of Florida into the Atlantic Ocean. The land surrounding the Halifax is lush with subtropical vegetation. Saw palmetto, mulberry, palm, magnolias, hickory, oak, pines, and cypress trees create a jungle of green. Along its shores, alligators bask in the sun. Turtles sun on logs. At dusk, bobcats, raccoons, white-tailed deer, and otters appear.

Halifax's average channel is eight feet deep. Close to shore, it can be two feet deep and as low as a foot. Overhead, blue herons, egrets, ospreys, pelicans, ibis, cormorants, bald eagles, and terns fly. The Halifax has brackish, semi-salt water with an abundance of fish: catfish, flounder, black drum, snook, redfish, bass, snapper, tarpon, sheepshead, and shellfish.

Lagoons form outside the main channel, creating a breeding ground for fish and other aquatic life. This is where John, Chase, Bella and I went fishing for redfish. The men had fished a lagoon the previous year, catching some good-sized redfish. (Redfish, copper in color with a black tail dot, are 16-18 inches and 30 inches long, weighing 5 pounds up to 7 or 8.) Pound for pound, redfish is one of the best fighting fish on the Atlantic. Redfish was what we were after!

Now, the Halifax has many lagoons. The men wished to fish in the same lagoon they fished last year. The only problem was our boat's draft was too long for the shallow waters. We could get stuck. John had a strategy. The trick to getting into the Redfish Lagoon was to take the boat out just as the water was coming out of its ebb to high tide, maybe two or three hours before a high tide, and ever so slowly and carefully move into the lagoon.

On a very cloudy day out, the boat was encased in thick misted vapor clouds; we could not see maybe three or four feet in front of us. The men fished, although they couldn't see where they were casting. Bella and I noted that we were in a cloud; we could see the water molecules with a dust-like appearance. The clouds lit up, and the water sparkled.

As the sun rose in the sky, eventually, the mist evaporated, and the clouds disappeared. The sky was fresh and blue. Bella, also known as "Eagle Eye," perused the upper heights of the trees on shore. A pelican flew in, encircling the boat. This pelican had been fed by other boaters and was looking for a handout. We enjoyed him. Pelican went round the boat, entertaining us, flying off and back again. Eventually, he flew away, slightly disappointed that his antics did not work.

With their fishing poles out, the two men used live shrimp as bait. (I was waiting to fish in the lagoon. Bella did not have a fishing license.) They were casting their lines in hopes that something would bite.

We waited for the tide to keep coming in so that we would have enough water depth to float the boat into the lagoon. We needed 1.6 feet. We had 1.3 feet but needed more; we were scraping the bottom.

Bella and I continued to absorb the river's natural beauty. Bella's eyes were fixed on the tallest tree on the shore across the river. She spotted an eagle.

Female bald eagles have about an eight-foot wingspan and weigh about 14 pounds (with males being somewhat smaller). They prey on waterfowl, small mammals, turtles, and roadkill. Perching in the tallest trees to spot their victims, eagles wait patiently. Their call is a high-pitched whistle, "*T-t-t-t-t-t-t-t...*" An eagle, whose vision is 4–8 times sharper than a human, can spot its prey close to two miles away.

I took out my binoculars and saw the eagle looking in the other direction. I could see its back. We were excited to see the bald eagle, who turned around and faced us. The eagle stayed stationed in position over us.

We continued quietly enjoying the beauty surrounding us, the clear blue sky, and the sounds of birds while the men kept casting their rods. Chase had his rod partially cast in the air on the side of the boat with shrimp bait hanging from the hook.

Out of nowhere, this bird, a Royal Tern, appeared. He looked like a thin seagull, black-capped with an orange beak, narrow light gray upper wings, white body, orange legs (weighing anywhere between 1–2 pounds, eight or nine inches long, and having a wingspan of about 20 inches. Plunge diving for fish is how terns feed for crustaceans, mollusks, and other invertebrates.) *Kee-yah!* is their cry.

The tern flew past John (at the bow), making a sharp left-hand turn to Chase (at the stern). The Tern dive-bombed at Chase. No! He is after the shrimp! We could not move fast enough. The energy rose in the boat. All attention went to the tern. We all held our focus on Chase.

In attempting to snatch the shrimp, the tern hooked his wing. Chase responded. He grabbed a washcloth to cover the eyes, but that did not work. It needed to be more significant. The tern was writhing and struggling to get free.

John threw Chase a hand towel. Chase was using his left hand to hold the tern, with the towel covering its eyes. The tern relaxed.

Gentle but firm without emotion, Chase removed the hook using his right hand with a pair of needle-nose pliers. Chase held the tern in his hands. With a few wiggles, the tern indicated it was time to go.

Chase released the tern. A bit shaken, the bird flew off. He landed in the water, wings spread out, head down with a slightly lifted chin, and started floating away from the boat. Then the tern began flapping his wings, and up into the air he rose, flying probably six feet. Tern down. I could see that the tern was pulling itself together. He tried flying again. Again, he drifted on the water. He disappeared out of our sight.

John, without a wake, guided our boat slowly, ever so slowly, leading us away—time to approach the lagoon. We may have moved fifty feet. Then something out of a *National Geographic* episode happened. That bald eagle, watching from his perch in the tree on the other side of the river, spread his wings and flew. Wow! Magnificent and majestic! We kept our eyes on him. Down he soared past our boat. The eagle briefly disappeared out of sight. Returning, the eagle had the tern in his claws and flew upward past us to the treetops and out of sight!

Tomorrow, the fishing will be better. There is no fish today.

Week 17: Embody Vibrational Energy

"If you want to find the secrets of the universe, think in terms of energy, frequency and vibration."

—Nikola Tesla

Guidance: First, take a moment to tune to the frequency of the present moment.

There is no static. Dial in to get a clear, strong connection. Remember how the radio dial between channels is static? Keep dialing in until you get that divine channel. For fun, let's call it "111". Focus your mind on the present moment.

Notice your physical sensations: warmth, coldness, tingling, happiness, sadness, or agitation. Take four deep breaths and invite the stillness of serenity in. Continue to breathe deeply and center your focus on the stillness. What do you observe now? Engage your senses: sight, sound, smell, taste, and touch. What sensations and feelings do you experience? Remain with the stillness and pay attention to any shifts or changes you notice.

Deep within your being lies a treasure awaiting discovery—your vibrational energy.

Deep within your being lies a treasure awaiting discovery—your vibrational energy. Vibrational energy is the energy that everything in the universe emits. It is a subtle energy that vibrates at different frequencies. This vibration permeates all living things, including you! When you join with your vibrational energy, you access a source of joy.

One of the most profound experiences you can have is finding and connecting with the vibrational energy within. It involves finding your tone and frequency and staying attuned to it. You become more attuned to it when you connect with nature, your creator, or the greater universe. This connection allows you to feel more centered and present.

Tuning in to this frequency helps you gain a new understanding. This heightened self-awareness lets you identify what truly brings you joy and peace. This vibration is Divine. By merging with it, you tap into your inner strength and resilience. This experience enables you to become more confident in your abilities, assuring you that you can face any challenges that come your way.

In opening to vibrational energy, you are open to myriad sensations, each unique to the individual experiencing them, and no two people will have the same experience. You may see your inner vibration as glowing, radiant, pulsating light of vibrant colors. You stay centered on the pulsating inner light, tuning up the body. As the energy current flows through each body cell, you may feel a softening or an electrical sensation. Others may experience this vibration through their other senses, possibly the taste ranging from sweet to bitter to metallic, the sound of *Mmm*, the aroma of a rose, or the softness of a flower petal. From this experience, you know a bit of bliss that aligns with your authentic self, tapping into you and your essence. This alignment brings about the flow in your life.

Realization: This knowledge can only be realized through personal experience.

When I reside in this energetic resonance, I feel peace and the fullness of my being. Fusing my mind and heart with my energy vibration enhances my intuition and ability to receive guidance. I become more attuned to my inner guidance, the subtle messages from the universe, and higher wisdom. This heightened awareness helps me to make better decisions and navigate life's journey with clarity and trust.

My understanding of my vibrational energy has deepened my awareness of vibrations. There are coarse vibrations and fine vibrations. Singing bowls have played a significant role in this discovery. The Singing bowls give me the experience of Oneness, connecting me to the All That Is. Singing bowls can be crafted to have a particular resonance to the octaves on the music scale. For instance, the F note carries the frequency of the heart chakra, which is believed to promote emotional well-being. Now, I see myself as a singing bowl radiating a particular vibrational energy based on the frequency I embody at any given moment. I am more mindful of the energy I am projecting into the world.

5 Keys to Knowing Your Vibrational Energy

1. Take a moment to check in with your body and become aware of your physical sensations.

2. Deep breathing and focusing on the still point create a sense of calm and presence.

3. Recognize that vibrational energy is the energy emitted by everything in the universe, vibrating at different frequencies.

4. You have your own tone and frequency of vibrational energy.

5. By tapping into your vibrational energy, you develop heightened self-awareness, which helps you identify what brings you joy and peace.

Moments of Embodying My Vibrational Energy

- I spoke on Applied Attunement at the Attunement Summit. My talk was extemporaneous. The substance of my talk was generated from my living. I trust that I said what I needed to say.

- I have made it my practice to review my day before bed. I find many things to be thankful for. I also forgive myself and others.

- I changed my thinking from "You probably don't want to" to "Here's something I'd like to do. Would you like to join me?"

- I started my day with a morning focus: light a candle, thank Divinity for my life, set an intention for my day, say a prayer, and sit in silence for four minutes, connecting with my inner vibration and sending love into the world.

- On Sunday, John and I participated in a Safe Peace Zoom Call, in which we were in the company of positive, uplifting people who sent radiant Light and Love for Safe Peace to the world.

- I played my note F singing bowl, which resonates with the vibrational frequencies of the heart chakra.

- I spent time with our juniper tree, appreciating its beauty and touching in with her vibrational energy.

Journal

How did you embody your vibrational energy this week? How do you think it can benefit you? Reflect and answer the questions.

Joyful Moments: Reflect and write freely from your heart about your weekly joy experience or any insights you may have.

Week 18: The Inner Garden and the Power of Trust

"What the world needs is more women who have quit fearing themselves and started trusting themselves."

—Glennon Doyle

Guidance: In the inner garden, the sanctuary within, you discover your true presence and the truth of love.

The world's external attractions, which tug at your heart, are seen for what they are. You feel their presence and hear their beckoning, but you do not respond. You do not reach out. You let them be, no matter how captivating they may seem. For instance, the pleading cries of your adult daughter cannot divert you from your inner peace. As the observer, you know they are not real; they are a part of the illusionary realm. Do not depart from the garden; it is within this sanctuary that the Divine resides. From here, everything can be held and handled. Do not react, fight, force, or flee. Be present with it. Breathe with it. Stay in the garden.

> *Do not react, fight, force, or flee. Be present with it. Breathe with it. Stay in the garden.*

As human beings, you are created from the earth with deep feelings and emotions, and you are a spirit being formed from Light and Love's essence, connected to the Source of all. To achieve wholeness, happiness, and health, navigating your emotional realm, recognizing it, and undertaking the necessary inner work is crucial. Your inner wisdom can guide you in self-reflection, and this process cannot be bypassed. Truth, forgiveness, and love—for you and others —are all integral parts of this journey. This wisdom was awakened by loss and grief, which is teaching you invaluable lessons.

The world's enticements themselves are not inherently bad or good. But, they have the potential to take you away from inner peace. They are distinctive to the individuality of the person. They work invisibly, like hypnosis, persuasively and slowly eroding the fiber of your being before you know it. What entices you? Examples of enticements are diverse and personal: excessive desire for material possessions, addictive use of social media and technology, worka-holism, unhealthy relationships, freedom from pain, wanting above all else for the family to be whole and happy, pre-occupation with world conditions, unhealthy lifestyle choices, hypocrisy—not living to your known integrity, freedom from accepting responsibility for what is and over-striving for perfection are just a few examples.

Anything that takes away inner peace, joy, play, and laughter is the lure. It is important to note that what disrupts inner peace for one person may not affect another similarly. Each individual's path to finding and preserving inner peace is distinct and necessitates self-awareness and deliberate decision-making. The best advice is to get in nature, connect and be with it, and get grounded in it. Balance returns, and so does inner peace.

Divinity attends to all the pulling of your heart from the depths of the inner peace garden. Once you depart from this sacred realm, you sever your connection with the Divine and become entangled in the web of existence that pulls at you. You merge with that which dissolves. You are then one with it. You no longer remain aligned with the creative process that emerges from the sanctuary of your inner garden. You cease to be a part of that which rises from the depths of your being. You have ejected yourself from the garden. It is up to you to meet the flaming sword to return to the garden.

Realization: I must remain focused on the present moment and respond with compassion.

I still face challenging circumstances that affect me. However, I choose to remain focused on the present moment and respond with compassion. It is difficult for me to understand certain situations fully. While I want to be supportive, becoming too deeply involved may interfere with the unfolding creative process. When I hold the challenge with love in my heart and trust that things are unfolding and the right outcome will manifest, I don't need to manipulate and fall into default habits of fear and worry.

I have noticed that the outcome remains the same when I end the creative process prematurely. It is a repeated pattern where my efforts lead to no real change. Everything seems to stay stagnant, except for the realization that what I am doing is not practical. It feels like I am just perpetuating the same situation. Now, I've started to listen to my inner wisdom and allow things to unfold naturally in their own time. I'm following that guidance.

I now choose to only engage in actions that serve the highest good. My mind may not understand the unseen realms, but I trust my inner guidance and the wisdom it offers. I rest in my heart, trusting the Divine, knowing the creative process is unfolding perfectly. My generation of spirit substance, created by Divine love and light, fuels the creative process to fruition.

When I fully trust in the creative process of the Divine, I have experienced an incredible transformation. I consistently find myself in the right place at the right time, engaging in suitable activities with the right individuals. I have a lengthy list of such experiences. Events unfold, and I do not need to intervene. I perceive what I need to see precisely when it is unveiled. I act when I sense an internal compulsion arising from a place of tranquility. My responsibility is to observe these dysfunctional patterns, emanate my light towards them, transmute them, allow love to perform its wonders. I will not and cannot forsake my inner sanctuary, allowing myself to be pulled away from my center. Otherwise, what I express is ineffective and fails to accomplish the purpose for which I arrived on this earthly plane. Through this approach, I embody peace and joy.

5 Keys to the Inner Garden and Trust

1. Discover True Essence.
2. Ignore External Allurements.
3. Non-Attachment.
4. Trust in the Divine.
5. Witnessing and Transmuting

Inner Garden Moments

- The book *Good to the Last Drop* with my chapter was published. I am feeling everything!

- I was offered an opportunity to lead a book club where *Good to the Last Drop* would be the first book to read. I'm feeling connected to something greater than myself.

- I posted about the book on Facebook and received good responses. I am happy.

- My son ordered *Good to the Last Drop*. I am feeling steady.

- I spoke with my editor, Mary Metcalfe, about creating *Journey to Joy* book. I am holding this cycle steady.

- My son and grandson visited us from Denver. I am feeling blessed.

- My life is in the flow. How can it get any better than this?

Journal

This week, what was your experience of your inner garden? Reflect and answer the question.

Joyful Moments: Reflect and write freely from your heart about your weekly joy experience or any insights you may have. Let your heart express itself through art.

Week 19: Uplifting Energy

"The only way to do great work is to love what you do."

—Steve Jobs

Guidance: Energy follows thought. Energy moves along the invisible light waves.

Energy works to create your thoughts. Love travels as light at the speed of light. Think of a loved one. Automatically, you connect to the light. Your heart lights up. Drop into your heart. Feel your internal atmosphere.

Please test it out. Think of an eagle. Pause. What do you feel? Think of an orchid. Pause. What do you feel? Pay attention to the energy surrounding the feeling. At this point of connection is an opportunity to radiate love/light into it. Now, feel the energy. You are strengthening the light that holds the world steady. It's as simple as that. You can do this with anything that comes up in your consciousness.

Realization: **The connection with earth and nature grounds me and connects me to Light and Love.**

I turn over what is beyond my control to the Grandmothers, who represent the spirit of the Divine. They provide love, support and wisdom in a way that is personal to me. Somehow, I feel their humanity. Perhaps it's because my grandmother was so dear to me. They help me connect with my spirituality beyond traditional beliefs. They are my guides who inspire and comfort me. Whatever I'm dealing with, I'm reminded that I gave it to the Grandmothers. Everything's working out, and it's no longer mine. There is no need to worry. I know this is true for me, and it works repeatedly. I'm doing the Grandmothers' work, and the Grandmothers are taking care of things out of my control. That mindset frees up the mind and heart to be in and stay in the present moment.

I have all the photos of my family on my bedroom wall: I have nine grandchildren and four children. First thing in the morning, I look at the wall before I get out of bed. I connect to each one through the Net of Light and send out love to them. I feel the whole Net of Light meditation in my body, with images in my mind radiating light from my heart. The Grandmothers are with me and their presence has transformed me. I have suffered in my life. Who hasn't? I lost my daughter to a senseless car accident. Now I have another daughter who is facing a severe illness. I am concerned that she is not taking care of herself as she should. These challenges gnaw at the fiber of a mother, right? I have given the things out of my control to the Grandmothers. This has freed me and uplifted my energy.

Anytime the mind goes to that weird thing of trauma: What's happening in the Earth? What's happening over there? Look what's happening. What's this kid doing over there? I breathe deeply, feel the net of light, think it in my body, and connect. It's a powerful tool the Grandmothers have given us. It is my primary tool.

The Grandmothers' path is the path of joy; follow the joy, the things that provide joy in my life. It works! Joyous choices appear all along the way. Choose joy. I think of the fairytale spreading the breadcrumbs, finding my way home. That's what the breadcrumbs are: joy crumbs guiding me home. I ask myself, "Do I resonate with this?" Keep following the joy. Keep following the Joy.

I have a friend who was suffering, and she took the joy path, and her joy was music. She started singing and singing and singing. She feels so much better now. So, I believe and know in the power of what I am doing. This practice is simple. I find it most powerful; the Grandmothers have made it easy for me and everyone on this path. It's a path of gratitude and joy.

5 Keys to Uplift Your Energy

1. I am embracing the concept of the Net of Light as a primary tool for staying in the flow of Life and experiencing upliftment.

2. I recognize the power of the Net of Light allowing one to surrender what is beyond one's control to a higher power.

3. I am cultivating a mindset of being present by freeing the mind and heart by giving my concerns to the Grandmothers or any form of the Divine.

4. It is understanding the transformative power of Joy and how it can positively impact physical and emotional well-being.

5. It recognizes that embracing the path of Joy can lead to uplifted energy, inner peace, and a smoother life navigation.

Uplifting Moments

- I went to a hospice volunteer social; positive present people.
- I connected with the net of light and did the meditation.
- I heard some funny stories about things tourists do and say.
- I celebrated my brother-in-law's 78th birthday with family and friends.

- I walked with a friend on the river trail.
- I worked in the garden, preparing the beds for planting.
- I visited with my daughter.

Journal

What uplifted your energy this week? Reflect and answer the question.

Joyful Moments: Reflect and write freely from your heart about your weekly joy experience or any insights you may have. Let your heart express itself through art.

Week 20: How Resilience Brings Joy

"Resilience is not about avoiding the obstacles, but about facing them head-on with unwavering strength and determination."

—Serena Williams

Guidance: Love unlocks resilience.

Love that has meaning and personally connects to the heart gives life, gives a current and a fire to live, gives purpose and inspiration, and knowing unconditional love opens the door to resilience. "You can only take a horse to water but you can't make it drink." Everyone who has ever been traumatized must eventually do the work for themselves without props, support, or goading. Everyone is on their own journey through life. You can have all kinds of hopes and wishes for another person. Once they are adults, their choice, their free will, determines the outcome.

Realization: Some people pick themselves up after trauma, and others get lost in it.

I read about resilient individuals whose early lives were disturbed by some disrupting adversity, such as parental death or abandonment, poverty, neglect, or abuse. They all grew and flourished. They overcame adversity with a creative outlet, a resilient mindset, a caring person, and an innate drive. What made them extraordinary was that they didn't become victims; they became the heroes of their stories. Their stories inspire me. If they can do it, others can, too. Life deals harsh circumstances. As my husband John always says, "Play the hand you're dealt." It is interesting to note that resilient people who took what life has given them made the best of it. They overcame their challenges and built inner strength. Despite their struggles, they did their work and didn't give up hope.

Getting one's needs met makes a significant difference in one's development. Think of Maslow's Hierarchy of Needs and how meeting the lower level to the higher levels leads to self-actualization. Here is the order of Abraham Maslow's hierarchy of needs, starting from the lowest level to the highest level: Physiological Needs, Safety Needs, Love and Belongingness Needs, Esteem Needs, and Self-Actualization Needs. In this order, physiological needs are the most basic, while self-actualization needs are the highest level of fulfillment. According to Maslow, self-actualization occurs when all needs are met. Could it be that having basic needs met stimulates resilience? This makes sense to me; from my experience, I know this to be true.

Resilience is an incredible trait. It is best when our parents guide us to the trait of resilience, being part of childhood development. Not all of us are lucky enough to have that parenting, so we figure it out independently. When we are resilient, we bounce back from challenges and become even more vital. I will examine some keys that help defy the odds and unlock resilience.

One of the essential keys to resilience is having our basic physiological needs met, as stated in Maslow's Hierarchy of Needs. It is a way to understand the factors that contribute to resilience. Each step builds upon the next step. Ultimately, reaching the pinnacle of self-actualization, the hierarchy shows us that fulfilling these needs is a solid foundation for resilience.

Another key to resilience is finding a creative outlet: art, music, gardening, dance, sports, nature, acting, anything that sparks the heart. It's the secret door that leads to inner strength and growth. It may take trial and error to ignite our path to creative expression. The power of creative expression is a magic wand that channels our emotions, finds our voice, and connects with others. Just like Albert Einstein and John Lennon did with their artistic pursuits, tapping into our imagination and being creative can foster resilience. Simple, but true.

Besides a creative outlet, having a support system is vital on this journey. Whether it's a caring person, a mentor, or a counselor, having someone who understands and listens without advising during tough times can make a difference. Active listening allows the speaker to be heard and feel understood. No matter how tempting, only advise if asked. When

> *Solving our problems develops confidence and self-dignity. When a problem comes to us, it is ours to solve, no one else.*

we think for others and solve their problems, we tell the listener they are not good enough or intelligent enough to figure things out for themselves. We are taking away their opportunity and dignity. Solving our problems develops confidence and self-dignity. When a problem comes to us, it is ours to solve, no one else.

Healing usually follows the support system and is integral to resilience. It means recognizing and addressing past traumas and fears. One way of making things right for oneself and others is Ho'oponopono.

I see a common thread within each of the four keys. That thread is Love; it connects us to the essence of life and gives us purpose and inspiration. It propels us forward on our life's journey to joy. Unconditional love fuels resilience and empowers us to navigate challenges with strength and grace.

A resilient mindset will eventually develop through the practice of a resilient attitude. It's all about seeing ourselves as the heroes of our stories rather than victims. As with nature, healing takes time and happens at its own pace. With a resilient attitude, we will meet challenges and use them as steppingstones to build strength—that's the spirit of resilience!

5 Keys to Resilience

1. Meeting basic physiological needs.
2. Finding a creative outlet.
3. A support system.
4. Healing past traumas and fears.
5. Developing a resilient mindset.

Resilient Moments

- I reflected and wrote about my past experiences.
- I had a heartfelt conversation with a person in hospice.
- I participated in a Safe Peace Community Zoom call.
- I completed my daily exercises.
- I tended my tomato, lettuce, and spinach plants.
- I wrote an unconditional love letter to my daughter.
- My friend and I discussed the power of unconditional love and forgiveness in healing relationships.

Journal

How did resilience bring you joy this week? Reflect and answer the question.

Joyful Moments: Reflect and write freely from your heart about your weekly joy experience or any insights you may have. Let your heart express itself through art.

Week 21: Life is Conspiring to Give Your Heart's Desire

"The future belongs to those who believe in the beauty of their dreams."

—Eleanor Roosevelt

Guidance: You create your own reality. What are your dreams?

What dream was placed in your heart before you were born? What is the dream you forgot as you grew to be an adult? What are you being called to remember? What dream resonates with your heart? Where is your life path taking you? Why do you ignore your heart's calling? Wake up! Life is calling you to wake up. Do what you came to Earth to do. This is how magical moments are born!

Look at your life, your world . . . you are getting what you have been unconsciously wishing for. You are invited to remember and open to your heart's dream.

Realization: When I have a desire, a great flush of appreciation flows through my body.

This is when I knew that my dream was coming from my heart. As a young girl, I wished to be in nature and have fun outdoors with my family. Unconsciously, I trusted the creative process. Whenever the opportunity connected to my dream arose, I took it. This thread brought me to the man I love: my marriage, living in Colorado, having a home in the mountains, and raising my family with a love of the outdoors. My dream became a reality for me. This dream is still unfolding.

I dream of writing and publishing a book which is in process. It took me time to realize my topic. I became aware of the emergence of this dream as things started to line up: conversations with John, Bonnie's guidance, journaling my healing process, and writing a chapter in Irene Weinberg's book. I pondered how I could generate funds for the Bonnie Albright Fort Lewis College teacher scholarship. Then, the inspiration came to me that I could turn my blog post about my healing joy journey into a book. The profits of this book will go towards her fund. This ignited a spark within me, propelling me on this exciting journey.

I have a few other heart desires in motion. I envision my body moving with ease. I dream of spending time in the most beautiful places in the world, untouched by man's development. My inner wisdom is in the background, guiding me in the unfoldment of my dreams.

Where once I saw problems as something to face, now I see them as opportunities unfolding. Keep looking up! When a problem arises, allow the opportunity to be revealed. Life is giving an opportunity. Life is teaching something.

> *When a problem arises, allow the opportunity to be revealed. Life is giving an opportunity. Life is teaching something.*

The true nature of life is change, giving, and loving. The ego mind cringes and fears, which keeps the opportunity from being unwrapped. No longer do I see a problem. Rather than seeing a problem, I now see this: something is presenting in my life that my programming has trained me to label it as a "problem" when it isn't a problem! I only perceive it that way. The "problem" is a signal to me that changes are afoot. An "opportunity" from the Great Spirit of Life is waiting to manifest through me. I need to pay attention, listen to my inner guidance, stay in my integrity, and do only what's mine. It's all about a change in perspective, an opening to learn and grow. My programming is in the process of being upgraded. As the door opens, joy walks in and my heart's desire transforms into a reality.

5 Keys to Seeing Opportunities

1. Shift from problems to opportunities.
2. Embrace change and uncertainty.
3. Listen to your inner guidance.
4. Stay in integrity.
5. Cultivate a growth mindset.

Moments with Opportunities

- I had a situation where my Zoom account was compromised when I gave someone else administration access. It was a learning experience for me.

- I discovered another more efficient, seamless way to deal with Situation #1, which doesn't require sharing my Zoom license.

- We bought a large mirror in Puerto Peñasco, Mexico, twenty years ago. It broke. Its match is on the other side of the bathroom counter. The first thought that came to me was, "It's replaceable." No big deal.

- My 24-year-old youngest daughter is moving to a new apartment. Moves can be stressful. In addition to that, she has an ear infection, cramps, and allergies, so she's feeling a lot. I listened. She can solve her problems. We did some breathing. Then, I shared a long-distance Reiki with her. We had a lovely time connecting. We both felt better sharing the attunement.

- I volunteer at the hospice house. My impaired hearing requires intense focus on the lips of the quiet, soft speaker, which exhausts me. I am listening to my needs. It is a volunteer position. A change is on the horizon.

- My opportunity to strengthen my body worked. My body is now solid and flexible. I am going to dance class on Thursday and kayaking at the lake on Friday! Woohoo!

- I sought mental clarity on a new concept and decided to write about it. As I put my thoughts into words, I experienced a sense of clarity and greater understanding.

Journal

Think about your heart's desire. How can you transform problems into opportunities for growth and change? Please reflect and answer the questions.

Joyful Moments: Reflect and write free from your heart about your weekly joy experience or any insights you may have. Let your heart express itself through art.

Week 22: Reflections

"In the process of letting go, you will lose many things from the past, but you will find yourself."

—Deepak Chopra

Guidance: You are going to do a little internal work this week.

Imagine clearing out the clutter of your inner sanctuary. Pull back the curtains and let the light in. Open the windows and feel the fresh air. Now sweep and dust. This is your sacred place. You will discern what to keep and what to let go of. You will bless that which goes and that which stays. Then, you will organize what remains. Imagine yourself sitting in the chair of your dreams. Look around. Are you satisfied? Do you feel inner peace? If not, take care of it.

You want your inner sanctuary to be a place of inner solace, peace, and tranquility—where you can reside undisturbed by the world's chaos. You disconnect from the external world and connect with your inner self. A refuge from the stresses and pressures of everyday life, a safe space for self-care, healing, and rejuvenation, this sanctuary is yours alone and is in your heart.

Realization: I must do my internal work. There is no getting around it.

Time for self-reflection. Let's review and answer these five questions over seven days:

1. What are your core values? Align your values with your goals.

2. How important are your current commitments? Align your commitments with your values.

3. What are your goals? Reassess them. Align them with your values.

4. How are you taking care of yourself? What is keeping you from self-care?

5. Why do you say yes to things that contradict your core values?

5 Keys to Reflection

1. Clearing out the clutter of one's inner sanctuary.

2. Discerning what to keep and what to let go of.

3. Blessing that which goes and that which stays.

4. Organizing what remains.

5. Creating a place of inner solace and peace.

Joyful Moments from Internal Work

- I realize I know who I am, my values, and my purpose.

- Being mindful helps me let go of any worries and experiences and embrace the beauty of the present moment.

- I am getting a clear vision of what is mine to direct and focus on.

- Being mindful helps me let go of worries about the past or future and embrace the beauty and joy of the present.

- I like painting; it helps me process my feelings in a creative and fun way.

- I love the quality of my friends and our friendship.

- I practice self-care by reminding myself of who I am and what I am here to be and do.

Journal

What reflections did you have this week? Reflect and answer the questions.

Joyful Moments: Reflect and write freely from your heart about your weekly joy experience or any insights you may have. Let your heart express itself through art.

Week 23: Communing with the Natural World

"The sun shines not on us but in us. The rivers flow not past but through us. Thrilling, tingling, vibrating every fiber and cell of the substance of our bodies, making them glide and sing. The trees wave, and the flowers bloom in our bodies and souls, and every bird song, wind song, and tremendous storm song of the rocks in the heart of the mountains is our very own song and sings our love."

—John Muir

Guidance: **For the next seven days, you will be communing with nature.**

Here are some reasons to spend time in nature: relaxation and stress relief; connection with the natural world; physical health benefits; mental and emotional well-being; inspiration and renewal.

Set a specific time each day for it. Be prepared with some form of a journal. Go out in nature. Observe. Get ready to receive a sensory reward. Let your creativity flow and use the writing tool that speaks to you. There are no strict rules for nature journaling. You can sketch, draw, and take notes. Do what comes naturally to you.

It's a beautiful time to nurture a deeper connection with nature. Begin with a child's curiosity. Discover a tranquil outdoor spot that calls out to you, then take a moment to settle in. Patiently wait until you connect with a specific plant, flower, tree, insect, animal, or rock. Approach it with gentleness, as if meeting a new friend. Sit quietly, breathe, and listen inwardly.

Observe keenly using all your senses—what does it look like, smell, feel like? Sketch or write down your observations. Reflect on your experience—what does this remind you of, how does it make you feel? Ask questions and record your thoughts. Finally, let your creativity flow—write a poem, sketch, or create something inspired by your encounter. This process deepens your bond with nature and opens doors to understanding its wisdom and beauty.

Realization: Tomorrow, I am going into nature for seven days.

I will be communing with nature. I will swim in the lake, hike the slick rock, kayak in the coves, view the sunrises and sunsets, sleep under the stars, watch the birds, connect with the plants, notice the insects, and look for stones. You and I will do the Nature Journal simultaneously. This journaling will be the first time I have kept my nature journal for an entire week to invoke peace and joy consciously.

"Keep some room in your heart for the unimaginable."

—Mary Oliver

5 Keys to Joy in Nature

1. Slow Down.

2. Be Present.

3. Observe and Listen.

4. Engage Your Senses.

5. Disconnect from Technology.

Joyful Nature Moments

I connected with the Canyon Spirit, the Water Spirit, the Wind Spirit, the Fire Spirit, the Earth Spirit, and the Spirit of the Ancients. I also connected with Grandmother Moon, myself, my light, and all my relations.

Journal

Write down the highlights of your nature journaling. How did Nature speak to you this week? Reflect and answer the questions.

Joyful Moments: Reflect and write freely from your heart about your weekly joy experience or any insights you may have. Let your heart express itself through art.

PART 4

FINDING WHOLENESS

You are all things. Denying, rejecting, judging or hiding from any aspect of your total being creates pain and results in a lack of wholeness.

—Joy Page

Cosmic Tapestry of Oneness

I have witnessed a dancing light web on the canyon walls of Lake Powell, as well as in the clear waters of Lake Nighthorse and the Caribbean. The Net of Light is real, tangible, and palpable. It serves as the vehicle for the interconnectedness of all life, becoming more vibrant as human beings generate love and truth. This light exists in every living atom; it is a fluid, transformative energetic force, strengthened by the radiance of love.

I learned about Attunement in 1979 from a local chiropractor. I had been experiencing migraine headaches. The chiropractor without touching me placed his hands in the energy field of each gland on the endocrine system. My headache disappeared. While I won't go into the details of the process, I found that whenever I received an attunement, I entered an energy field of light and love. In those moments, I was completely present, my mind was still, and I felt a sense of balance and alignment.

Eventually, I received training in Attunement. Initially, I practiced only on my immediate family and friends, without any charge. However, as my family grew and my career progressed, I stepped away from sharing attunements. Instead, I began to apply the principles of energetic attunement to my everyday life. This allowed my life to flow with grace, and I noticed that I could think of someone and then receive a phone call from them just seconds later. I would need something and it would come to me almost effortlessly. This left me wondering how these synchronicities happened.

It made perfect sense to me that these experiences were manifestations of light and love. I was content with that explanation. When I connected with the Grandmothers, I learned about the Net of Light, and the imagery and concept resonated deeply with me. It enhanced my ability to be in the present moment. It was like a revelation—this is how light works. My heart became the connector. Knowing that energy follows thought, it all made sense to me. While this may seem abstract to many, it works in my life, and it sparked a desire in me to research more and learn about the Net of Light.

Initially, I began writing this essay to clarify my jumbled thoughts on energy work, the chiming singing bowls, the Attunement healing practice, and the Net of Light. As my writing process unfolded, it became clear that I needed to explore and articulate the concept of energy and its relationship to a light infrastructure and oneness. I hope you find this exploration as valuable as I have.

What is the relationship between the Net of Light and energy? Energy exists in everything. If energy permeates all, then what is the connecting framework? Throughout this essay, this infrastructure is referred to by various names, with the predominant term being the Net of Light. This framework not only describes the essence of energy but also illustrates how it unifies us all.

Increasingly, people are becoming aware of a network that transmits vibrations, frequencies, tones, and energies. My interest in singing bowls and their profound positive effects on my intentions led me to study vibrational tones, notes, sounds, and their energies. The energies that exhibit vibrations and frequencies include sound, light, movement, heat, and even the tiniest atomic particles. I understand that energy cannot be created or destroyed; it can only be transformed from one form to another. Human beings possess the unique ability to transform energy through their thoughts, words, and feelings, leading to innumerable ramifications.

I recognize that energy can be connected, conserved, renewed, transformed, and measured—the first four characteristics being fundamental to the Net. As I grow more familiar with the Net of Light, I discover that each new understanding opens further avenues. My deep knowing increases, awakening me to limitless possibilities. This journey of understanding reveals the depth of connection that the Net of Light embodies.

Energy can be connected, conserved, renewed, transformed and measured.

From my perspective, the concepts of Attunement, Divine Unconditional Love, Reiki, Energy, Life Force, Chi, Breath, Divine Light, Essence, Spirit, Grandmothers, Ancestors of Light, Love, and Radiance—along with countless other names representing the vibration and frequency of love's light—are all encompassed within this light construct. This web of relationship further illustrates the unity of all existence.

In the latter part of my life, I have faced sorrow. It was my connection with the Net of Light, sending love and light into my circumstances and personal struggles, that transformed my perspective and approach to life. Love and joy emerged, shifting my focus from doing to being. I no longer see 'problems' but recognize 'opportunities' to send love through the Net of Light.

Here's how it works: Test it out. Think of someone you deeply love. Pause. What do you feel? Now think of a friend. Pause. What do you feel? Pay attention to the energy surrounding those feelings. At the point of connection lies an opportunity to radiate love and light into it. Feel the energy; you are strengthening the light net that holds the world steady. It's as simple as that. You can apply this practice to anything that arises in your consciousness.

This process of transmutation has shifted my challenges into blessings. Now, I take care of myself and engage in what is mine to do. This approach fosters a more balanced life, freeing me from the weight of the world. Like an eagle soaring high, I gain vision and see the light of life all around me.

The Net of Light has transformed my viewpoint on life. Initially, it felt magical. However, I came to understand that it is the framework of energy facilitating the experience of oneness and synchronicity. While conducting some research online, I came across a reference to Martin Exeter, one of my mentors from 1979 to 1988. He spoke of a network forming, "casting a net over the world, a net of control and containment, dominion and containment." In that moment, I felt I was being guided.

Awakening to Oneness

I believe Bonnie is here. I have experienced her presence repeatedly; therefore, I know she is here. With each experience, my trust in her presence grows stronger. When I believe in something and have firsthand experiences of it, I begin to know it deeply. This truth — "you know what you experience"—applies to various situations and interactions with others. It evolves from belief into a profound knowing.

I seek a deeper understanding of why I sense my daughter's presence beyond her earthly existence. I have felt her presence in nature—the clouds, birds, trees, sunrises, sunsets, full moons, night sky, deer, foxes, eagles, and hawks. These elements serve as glimmers of her essence and provide me with an experience of Bonnie in the present moment. It is undeniable: she helps us, her family, and her good friends. I turn to her for guidance, and the help arrives. When I think of her, my experience brightens. These God Winks from her lead me to contemplate the transcendence of mortal existence and the reality of life after death.

How is it that my daughter communes with me while she is no longer in her body? From the moment Bonnie was born, she brought light into our lives. She never met a stranger. In the last seven years of her life, Bonnie focused on what she came here to realize and transmute. In the three years before she departed this earthly plane, everything was manifesting for her. Radiance and light defined her; Bonnie knew who she was.

Our relationship was one of mother-daughter light. I understood her light identity. Bonnie flowed with Life, and I believe she connected with her Higher Self. Her life reflected this connection, resulting in synchronistic events. She called upon her heavenly grandparents for help and support, and they answered her prayers. This was evident in her life: a full college scholarship, a teaching position, and a home—she attracted what she desired. Now, Bonnie lives on in the celestial realm. She is part of everything and continues to connect with me in the present moment. I am motivated to remain present in the present moment to maintain a connection with Bonnie, not based on memories. A new light relationship with her unfolds. We are not limited by time or space; our current relationship is based on where we both are now. Even though I call her my "Light Daughter," we are spirit to spirit, not mother to daughter.

Bonnie is one with Source. Source reveals and originates the inherent unity of all things. We can call this "oneness," which is an understanding of why we sense God. In this space, I realize that my roles, thoughts, feelings, or emotions do not define me. Instead, I am the Higher Self observing my capacities of mind, heart, and body. The Higher Self speaks through my mind, heart, and body. When my capacities align with my higher purpose, I experience a state where earthly constraints, frustrations, and chaos lose their power over me. I resonate with the words: "None of this moves me."

If this is true for me, it may be true for you. Now, together we will explore the idea that Love and Light remain the sole enduring essence after physical death and examine the relationship between enlightenment, divine reality, and the eternal nature of Love.

The state of being resides in our inner garden, our internal sanctuary of peace. This state of existence transcends ordinary human experience or understanding. It is a consciousness in which we rise above our limitations and connect to something greater than ourselves. Although the world may be in chaos—filled with lies, hate, division, suffering, violence, war, and starvation—we can draw from our inner peace to meet these challenges.

In this state, we see with new eyes. We release our programming and touch the truth of ourselves. We gain insights into the nature of our reality, our true selves, and our purpose on Earth. This transformative experience leads to personal growth and spiritual awakening, which includes an awakening to the truth of life. Our hearts soften, and we become more compassionate, kinder, and wiser. Living in the present moment, we see our experiences as serendipitous, reflecting that things are working out just right. We are playing our unique part—no one else can do it quite like us.

Our focus determines where we direct our energy. Just as I concentrate on the love and connection I share with Bonnie, perhaps we can change our world by collectively focusing on harmony and understanding. When we align our personal intentions with the broader goal of societal unity, we create a powerful force for change.

Some individuals remain oblivious to their inherent divine nature, which has been working undercover. I am reminded of the Arab proverb:

He who knows not,
and knows not that he knows not,
is a fool; shun him.

He who knows not,
and knows that he knows not,
is a student; teach him.

He who knows,
and knows not that he knows,
is asleep; wake him.

He who knows,
and knows that he knows,
is wise; follow him.

Upon leaving this physical world, the unacknowledged divine identity departs without experiencing its complete love embodiment. The body returns to the earth, but the Light/Love lives on, remaining connected to its love connections. It does not matter if the earthly connection knows it or not. However, it is a great blessing when a human being recognizes it.

Mortal existence is often considered an illusion due to its fleeting nature and attachment to material possessions. In simple terms, the existence of form is an illusion because it doesn't last forever, distracting us from our true nature. The form itself is acceptable, but problems arise when we focus on the material world and lose sight of why we are here on Earth. When the form is put to the right use, it is beneficial. However, when our minds focus solely on form, it becomes problematic. Fear, anxiety, anger, envy, disappointment, complaints, blaming, and addictions emerge. People often exhibit behaviors driven by the absence of Love, such as egoism, greed, and self-interest. It is essential to recognize that these behaviors are impermanent and cease to exist upon the death of the physical body. What truly endures beyond death is not the accumulation of material wealth or worldly achievements, but rather the essence of Love itself.

Love is both eternal and divine. It surpasses the limitations of mortal existence and extends beyond physical death. Love is not bound by time, space, or the constraints of the material world. Instead, it resonates at an eternal and divine frequency, allowing individuals to awaken to their true essence and experience oneness.

The Divine Essence endures beyond death. We see this by connecting the threads of awakening to our true self, our divine reality, and the eternal Love. When we awaken and merge with our divine self, we rise above mortal existence and experience only the physical death of our body. Behaviors arising from the absence of Love cease to exist, leaving behind only Love's everlasting divine frequency. Love is the eternal essence that surpasses the boundaries of the earthly plane. Light, which carries the current of Love, connects all Life.

I wrote this essay to give credence to the reservoir of realizations and insights that have been bubbling up inside me. I needed to express them for mental clarity. This essay serves as a platform for me to articulate and share these experiences and understandings, allowing them to be heard and acknowledged. Through the process of writing, I have gained a deeper understanding of why I sense my daughter's presence beyond her earthly existence. I have explored the connection between her presence in nature and the help she provides to her family and friends. I have delved into the concept of oneness with Source and the transcendence of mortal existence. I have awakened to the truth of life and the enduring essence of love.

I have come to realize that human existence is an illusion and that Love is an eternal, divine frequency that surpasses the limitations of physical death. In conclusion, I can confidently say that my beloved Bonnie is eternal, and there is no death, only a metamorphosis.

Week 24: Yin and Yang, Exploring the Feminine and Masculine Energies

"Masculine and feminine energies are not limited to gender. They are present in all of us, and it's important to honor and embrace both sides."

—Brené Brown

Guidance: **The fluidity between Yin and Yang principles has revealed a harmonious balance, where the strengths of both energies complement and enhance one another.**

Yin and Yang have nothing to do with gender. They transcend it. Both principles arise as needed in both genders. There is a flow between Yin and Yang that finds harmony. The more Yang there is, the less Yin there is, and vice versa. Where there is war and violence, this indicates there is too much Yang and a deficit of Yin. As Yin increases, Yang decreases. The energies are designed to synchronize in a harmonic dance. Yang is evident in direction and focus. Yang is assertive, confident, focused, and proactive. The mind is engaged. Yang embodies strength, courage, protection, logic, and reasoning. Additionally, it can infuse a person with confidence, independence, and leadership.

Yin empowers collaboration, creativity, and a wholistic perspective. This energy represents a receptive and intuitive approach to life, emphasizing the significance of emotional intelligence and under-standing. Yin is a balancing force to the yang's action-oriented and assertive energy. It is a beautiful, powerful, life-giving force. Without Yin, you would burn yourself out.

Realization: Each of us is evolving and growing.

I am learning about Yin Yang. I didn't think much about Yin Yang until someone told me we would not discuss them. It must be against her religion and made her uncomfortable. Intrigued, I became more curious and read about Yin Yang. I can see nothing wrong with them. I will not mention Yin Yang to this person.

As an elder and grandmother, I knew of Yin, the energy of the feminine principle. Until recently, I had never considered Yang, the energy of the masculine principle, as it related to me. I only projected thoughts of yang onto my husband or my son. In a time when people are questioning their masculinity and femininity, internally and externally, I decided to contemplate Yang to see how the energies have played a role in my life.

Yang has been at play throughout my life, often without my conscious recognition. I was and am comfortable with these mas-culine principles and energies as I embody them. Yang frequently supported me in my day as I participated in my responsibilities that required me to act, lead, make decisions, and exert control over what was mine to do. There were also moments when I tapped into my masculine energy, being dominant, focused, assertive, and exercising control over my world. I get things done. I can be a force of nature. My yang stripes protect myself, my family, my friends, and my area

Mother Earth, as does Yin, emphasizes the oneness of all beings.

of service—more examples of the flow and weaving of Yin and Yang energies in my lifetime.

My critical life decision-making has always been guided by my heart, utilizing the energy of the Yin. When choosing my life partner, for instance, I followed the guidance of my heart, which brought me to a perfect match. As a mother, like many mothers, I embodied nurturing, compassion, and kindness. The feminine principle has worked with me throughout my life, often without my awareness. Mother Earth, as does Yin, emphasizes the oneness of all beings. Yin has shown me the importance of nurturing and caring for myself and others. In my work as a special educator, I drew upon the energies of the feminine principle, which include understanding, creativity, compassion, and intuition. Until recently, I was about the latter, caring and encouraging others. In my elder years, Yin has drawn me to self-care, filling myself with Yin to offer my energy to others.

Reflecting on my journey, I realize that integrating masculine and feminine energy principles has shaped my life and personality. Embracing my yang energies has empowered me to recognize the immense significance of my energetic passion, igniting a fire within me to pursue personal and professional growth with unwavering enthusiasm.

5 Keys to Yin and Yang Energies

1. Yin and Yang transcend gender.
2. Yang represents assertiveness and focus.
3. Yin embodies receptivity and intuition.
4. The balance between Yin and Yang is essential for harmony.
5. Integration of Yin and Yang shapes personal growth.

Moments of Yin Yang

- John and I went food shopping.
- We participated in a mix gender gym class.

- We ate lunch at our favorite local restaurant.

- We bought cherries and peaches from the Peachy fruit stand. I had a pleasant conversation with the clerk.

- We watered plants.

- I practiced sound healing with rattle, drum, singing bowl, and chimed.

- We harmonized on our Alaska trip.

Journal

How does Yin and Yang work in your life? Please reflect and answer the question.

Joyful Moments: Reflect and write free from your heart about your weekly joy experience or any insights you may have. Let your heart express itself through art.

Week 25: Oneness and Harmony

"Oneness is a deep feeling of connection, of harmony, of form and formless being One."

—Elsie Spittle

Guidance: Refer to Part 4, "The Cosmic Tapestry of Oneness." When you are in a state of love, you vibrate at a higher frequency.

This elevated vibration creates an energetic field that resonates with a higher frequency. Think of a time when you felt deep love or compassion, perhaps with a loved one or in nature. In those moments, you experienced lightness, joy, and glimmers of everything around you, resonating with the same frequency. This is your vibrational frequency at work harmonizing with love.

Allow your whole body to feel this comforting energy. Feel peace, assurance and clarity. Let it lift you above earthly devastations, lies and horrors. Now feel your heart. Think about who is suffering and maintain your inner peace. This is the way to hold those you love in your heart without losing your peace and getting emotionally attached to the chaos of the world. If any uncomfortable feelings arise, relax with them. Feel the feelings. They cannot hurt you. They will pass. Keep your position and a higher perspective. Know all is well. Stay connected to your higher self, align with your inner wisdom, and feel a sense of safety, security, stability, and resilience within your energetic field. When disaster approaches, apply this same healing energy. As Jesus said, "Be in the world, but not of it."

Realization: **I realize the universality of the Light and Love and its interconnectedness with all that is.**

I have reviewed scientific research that provides evidence of this connection including Wood Wide Web, Web of Life, Epigenetics, Neural Network, Biophoton Communication, Mycelial Networks, the Biospheric Ecosystem and Adaptive Resilience. Through these studies, it becomes clear that is no separation, only oneness.

As I face these challenging times, I am held in an energy that loves and supports me. According to quantum physicist, David Bohm stated, "The individual is not separate from the whole, and our actions have an impact on everything around us." Since I am connected to the whole, I can allow my light to bring harmony to the entire planet. As time unfolds, I trust that I will witness a beautiful outworking of this interconnectedness. Trust the process. This network and its many harmonizing aspects help me keep centered and grounded during these times of change.

As I reflect on the interconnectedness of all life, my new thought is that divisiveness stems from a state of mind. I recognize that the division has been created by the thoughts of humans. In contrast, the natural world. demonstrates a diversity of characteristics that contribute to the balance in nature. Each member is accepted as it. No two are identical. Each plays a particular role in the balance. I revel in the possibilities of humanity finding balance.

5 Keys to Oneness

1. Inclusivity and balance.
2. Embracing diversity.
3. Coexistence.
4. Focused energy.
5. Shifting perspective.

Moments of Oneness

- I went to the Canyon of the Ancients and attended a concert by Carlos Nakai and Will Clipman. The setting and music were stunning, and I felt harmony.

- In my first longevity class, I failed to pace myself. The following two days, I paid the price. I felt out of balance.

- I missed two events due to physical exhaustion. I shifted my perspective.

- I paced myself and listened to my body. The second longevity gym class improved because I focused my energy and listened to my body.

- John and I celebrated our 52nd wedding anniversary. We had an excellent time at home. We watched our 50th wedding anniversary video. We had a nice dinner and had a good conversation.

- I went kayaking. It was a beautiful day. Clouds were in the sky. The water was clear and calm, and we were there at the right time. I felt relaxed and balanced.

- The "no-see-ums"—tiny bugs that came out and bit me when the temperature reached the 90s— left me with huge welts all over my calves. It's taken a lot of self-discipline not to scratch my bites. I caved many times. I embraced my itches.

Journal

Explore and reflect on Oneness in you and in your world. How do you experience harmony or oneness in your living? Write about it.

Joyful Moments: Reflect and write freely from your heart about your weekly joy experience or any insights you may have. Let your heart express itself through art.

Week 26: Awakening to Oneness

"In the midst of chaos, there is also opportunity for growth and unity."

– Dalai Lama

Guidance: Refer to Part 4, "Awakening to Oneness." Fill yourself with warmth and connection.

Embrace the essence of love and unity, for even in the face of loss, you can find strength and light. You are invited to feel the presence of your loved ones, transcending the boundaries of time and space. Seek the light within yourself, allowing it to guide you toward deeper understanding. Recognize the enduring nature of love, for it is the thread that binds all existence and connects you to the divine.

Realization: I hope this book sparks contemplation, reflection, and a deeper connection to the Divine within each of us.

May it serve as a reminder that Love is eternal and that by embracing our true essence, we can transcend the learned limitations of human existence and experience the beauty and interconnectedness of all life.

5 Keys to Awakening to Oneness

1. Experiential Knowing.
2. Connection with Higher Self and Nature.
3. Embracing Love as the Enduring Essence.
4. Inner Peace and Expanded Awareness.
5. Harmony in Diversity.

Joyful in Awakening to Oneness Moments

- Cooking dinner.

- Spending time with John.

- Expressing my emotions through art.

- Dancing to my favorite music.

- Facing opportunities with a positive attitude.

- Practicing mindfulness meditation.

- Volunteering to help with an event.

Journal

What personal experiences have you had that deepened your understanding of oneness, and connection with others? How can you nurture those connections in your daily life?

Joyful Moments: Reflect and freely write from your heart about your weekly joy experience or any insights you may have. Let your heart express itself through art.

PART 5

GRIEF IS A FRIEND

"Grief can be a burden, but also an anchor. You get used to the weight, how it holds you in place."

—Sarah Dessen

Remembering a Life Filled with Passion and Love: My First Adult Experience with Deep Grief

My mother, father, two sisters, nephew, and I converged in Seattle, Washington, to be with my brother in his last days. The doctor said that my brother had only a few weeks to live. Feeling a bit uncomfortable because of the circumstances and the fact that we had not been together like this for some twenty years, we were all on edge.

As long as I have known my brother, he was passionate. Whatever he did, he did with his whole life's passion, allowing it to possess his being. Determined to master what life put in front of him . . . the German language, wrestling, mechanical, electrical, and aeronautical engineering, international sales, and cancer were no exception. With cancer, my brother had lost everything: his job as a mechanical engineer with Westinghouse, his marriage, his house, his insurance, and his health.

His new business, "Maya," which means "no material possessions" in Hinduism, focused on his new state of being. Disabled, living in a small one-bedroom apartment, my brother had discovered yoga, meditation, and Eastern philosophy. Before us was the metamorphosis of a transparent, transcendent guru.

The center point of the living room was the hospital bed. Just a few feet away sat my brother. His scalp reflected light like a freshly cleaned whiteboard. His body was pale white and soft, reminding me of an older man in his eighties. Could this be my brother, just forty-six years old? How could this have happened to him? A clear plastic tube attached to his nose was connected to a respirator. A continual whoosh with each draw indicated my brother's struggle to breathe. Yet beyond all this, the grin of a Cheshire cat gleamed on his face.

From there, as if we were tourists, my brother showed us Seattle. We walked the Japanese gardens and ate seafood at a nearby open-air restaurant. A few days passed, and we took walks in his neighborhood.

It was a time of loving connection and being together as a family. All the while, we avoided the topic of death.

Knowing full well that his days were numbered, I asked him, "What can I do for you?"

My brother's eyes brightened, "I want to celebrate Father's Day."

I paused as if I had auditory processing problems. Questioning his response, I awkwardly replied, "Father's Day isn't until June 17th. It's June 1st."

Again, my brother said, "Yes, I want to celebrate. I want a celebration with our family. I am going to miss Father's Day. Yes, Father's Day! Can you do that?"

"Sure," I replied, "What do you want?"

"All of us to be in one room, probably my bedroom. Pull down the shades. We will sit in a circle. Oh! Get candles and M&M's."

"What else?" I inquired. (When we were little, my dad occasionally brought home an attaché case filled with M&Ms from his client.)

"You'll see," he answered with a twinkle in his eye.

I did just what he told me to do. My sister thought he must be crazy for wanting to have a party. Initially, I felt this was a great idea, but now I was beginning to doubt my brother's judgment. I picked up candles, streamers, and candy at the local drugstore. That evening, after dinner, my sister and I arranged the room just as he requested.

As if we were dead men walking, the five of us stoically filed into my brother's candle-lit bedroom. Then it hit me like a bullet.

Thoughts rushed through my head, "What are we doing here? My heart is breaking. My brother is leaving us, and he wants to have a party. I did not want this! None of us did! We should just all sit and cry!"

Seated, we all turned to my brother. In silence, he looked at us with love. We returned that loving look and turned to each other. Then, my brother began.

"I know this isn't Father's Day, but this is my Father's Day celebration. I want each one of us to express our feelings to Dad and recall any special memories of him. I will go first. Dad, I appreciate how you stuck with me in Little League even when I could not hit or catch the ball. You kept rooting for me. Thanks for steering me into wrestling. I was getting so frustrated with baseball.

"You kept me away from bad influences. Remember Eddie Smith. . . When Sister Mary refused to recommend me for Loyola, you directed me to Polytechnic.

"You pushed, and I pulled. I always wanted to do the opposite of what you wanted. You never gave up on me. You were always there for me. I love you, Dad."

Turning to his son, "My son, I hope I've been a good father. I tried my best. I love you. I will always be with you, no matter where I am. Let Grandpa help you. Listen to him."

Looking at my father, he said, "Dad, be a father to my son."

Next, it was my turn. Gulp! "Oh! Dad, I thought I was the only one who couldn't catch a ball . . ." Each of us, in turn, gave our appreciative responses to our father.

Dazed, my nephew spoke, "I love you, Dad." Spoken last, those words released the floodgates. My brother froze and extended his hands like Jesus, calming the turbulent waters. Calm filled the air; we all stopped.

With reassurance, my brother responded, "You'll be okay. You will all be okay. Please do not wait for me to die. Go home."

The next day, my mother, father, and sisters left. My nephew and I remained. In the few days that followed, I saw my brother diminish quickly. It became apparent he could not care for himself. My brother wanted to me to stay with him through his transition process. Since it was summer and school was out, I could stay with him without pressure to return home. I consulted with my dear friend, Roger, on how to proceed and hold this transition process.

Shaving, bathing, and cooking were no longer independent activities. Hospice came. My brother joked with the caregiver. Realizing he could no longer care for himself, the presence of hospice elevated the already present tension.

Finally, the time came. We were ready but not ready. That night, the tube was annoying him. Deep, intentional breathing started. His irritation ceased. My brother moved into an altered state in what seemed like geologic time. He murmured about lifetime experiences; his life was passing before him. We prayed with him.

My brother's girlfriend and I connected closely with Hospice about the unfolding. We were to administer morphine when he was in pain. Nothing we were doing seemed to aid his process. The Hospice nurse advised us to bring my brother to the Hospice House.

The Hospice van arrived. Laying on the gurney went my brother. His girlfriend and I were at his side. His son followed us in his car.

When we arrived at the Hospice House, my brother was wheeled to his room. The room felt peaceful. It seemed like heaven to me. We were only there for minutes when a shift of energy happened.

At four in the morning, stillness permeated the air. For a split second, a white light illuminated the room. Peace filled our beings. The light went dim. My brother was gone.

Joy in Making Grief My Friend

The following excerpt is from my chapter, "My Path to Joy" in the book entitled *Good to the Last Drop* by Irene Weinberg.

In my story, you will learn how I am maneuvering through the third chapter of my Life: how I became friends with grief, what I learned, and how I managed it. It is my path to joy.

The Transformative Power of Love

The biggest realization I received at the onset of my path to joy was this: everyone is on their own journey, even our children. What I tell you here is what I did. It doesn't necessarily mean it works for you. It is my journey. It was designed especially for me. You will have your journey. When a loved one 'dies' and this person has been a daily part of your Life, Grief shows up, ferociously leveling you. This person came through your birth canal. You nursed this person as a baby. You fed, bathed, taught, laughed, and cried with this person. You watched this person grow and develop into a positive, loving being. This person was a bright light in your life. You watched this person face and handle with integrity as best as possible all the earthly struggles: accidents, divorce, men, single parenting two sons, and struggles with finances. You saw this person have one victory after another, facing these struggles and being a light in her world with almost everyone she met. You get a clue that your cord of connection is beyond just an earthly one.

Embracing Mindfulness and Healing

In the last year of this person's life, this person graduated from college with honors. This person taught 6th grade Science, Math, and Mindfulness. This person loved nature and the outdoors. In two separate incidents, I saw her rescue an injured hawk and an uncrewed motorboat on the lake. She liked fermenting foods, eating salads, and raw garlic too. She camped, hiked, backpacked, paddle boarded, kayaked, played basketball, and made jewelry and salves. She loved her sons more than anything else in the world. She loved children, and children loved her. She had this unique way about her; whatever she got became beautiful, unique, and valuable. She was beautiful and radiant. She had perfect posture. She never met a stranger. She was independent. I could go on and on. I love this person so much! This person is my daughter, Bonnie Jeanne Albright.

The Continued Presence of Bonnie

I felt this deep, dark, empty place within myself. I felt like I could not go on without her. I was living without her Bonnie form on earth. For a time, I could do very little. I came to know that love never dies. Love is eternal. Bonnie was ever present with me. Changing my thinking, I began to heal. Don't feel sorry for me. It is what it is. The thought of Bonnie being gone left me lifeless. My body froze. My body was a walking gravestone. I had many things to deal with and needed support. Included in this list were Bonnie's two sons, my physical health, my disabled daughter, and coping with daily life under the strain of Grief. I had to heal myself. I had other children and my grandchildren. I had to get back into life. I am not a victim, so I embrace what is. I came to know that love never dies. Love is eternal. Bonnie is ever present with me. Changing my thinking, I began to heal. I prayed to Bonnie. I started hearing her. Not in the usual way one hears things, but I knew it was her speaking to me. She was coming from my heart.

Reconnecting with Nature and Community

I began to fill my life with all the things that she loved. I thought about everything she loved and what she did that brought her joy, and how she healed herself. My thought that was in pursuing all the things that Bonnie loved, little by little, I could take steps to bring Bonnie back into my life. Then I will find Bonnie. It worked. Bonnie brought Mindfulness to me, so I put Mindfulness in my life. I took two mindfulness series and continued my practice daily, which started my journey back to myself. Through meditation, I realized I was not my mother self. I was the observer of the mother self. I began to have compassion for my mother self. I started to send my love for Bonnie to every cell of my body. My body healed. Even years later, I am still on this course. Mindfulness Meditation has been a gift that helps me navigate Grief. I was lucky to be with Bonnie for thirty-six years on earth. It may be the hardest thing I have ever done.

Finding Joy Amidst Sorrow

The change in our relationship from the physical to the spiritual plane was the answer for me. She is still present with me. As things proceeded, I found what follows to be true. I am continually having experiences of Bonnie actively involved in my life. I know that Bonnie is part of my spirit team. She is ever-present. Bonnie comes to my assistance eager and willing. Even with all these new insights, I couldn't ignore Grief, push her away, or block her out by being busy or sick. Eventually, she found her way back in. Grief was persistent. I had to listen to her. She kept telling me I was stuck and had not done all my work. There was more for me. I wasn't going back to the way things used to be. Friendships and interests shifted. She was requiring more from me. There was nothing else I could do. I embraced Grief.

A New Way of Being

Grief became my friend. First, Grief spent lots of time with me. Over time, we got to know each other well. Then, I invited Grief at a chosen time for a daily hourly visit. I would be with her. Grief liked to play games. She masked as depression or unrest. Eventually, I came to understand her and knew what she wanted. She wanted me to go deeper into my inner world to view something with me. The sooner I did this, the better it was for me. Sometimes, Grief wanted me to be still. Connect with nature. Be creative. We had fun being together. Over time, my compassion and understanding grew. My appreciation for everything grew. I found joy again.

Opportunities for Change

Grief rarely visits anymore, but when she does, I welcome her. I am present to receive what she brings. Grief makes me a better, wiser, and more loving person. Grief is one of the gateways to the experience of unconditional Divine Love. The grief process has connected me with something far grander than I could have ever imagined. I have found my inner voice, my inner guidance. I realize that Bonnie is still with me as light. She is now my light daughter.

The Path to Joy: A Lifelong Journey

I started to get signs and messages. They brought me comfort and gave me life to continue living. Following my heart, my love for Bonnie led me to joy. I found her in the present moment. And I stay in the present moment. Being with Bonnie has brought renewed interest in living and appreciating the things of life. Bonnie got me back to Mother Earth. Mother Earth told me, "Now you know how I feel." Those words shot through me! I took her words to heart. Her words motivated me to action. My life transformed. I began to commune with nature and sing. I studied Ho'oponopono. I utilized breathing to process what came up in my feeling realm. My husband and I started the Bonnie Albright Fort Lewis College Teacher Education Scholarship for single mothers. I went to grief counseling and a grief support group.

A dialogue between John and me; we recall the shift in the relationship from daughter in form to daughter in Spirit, Light Daughter.

John: "I have been thinking about something related to our previous topic of long breathing. One of the best things I could have ever heard was what a friend told me when we moved Bonnie's stuff from her house to ours. This friend had recently lost his adult son in an avalanche. He said, "Breathe deep!"

Anita: "I remember."

John: "He was telling me this. The secret is to breathe deep!" I thought, "Yeah, right!" When the grief came on, I remembered his words. I remember him saying, "Breathe deep." I did it! What that did for me is at some point, I started realizing that when I breathe deep, I was breathing in Bonnie's essence."

Anita: "Yes, yes!"

John: "Then it became almost routine and my practice. Whenever I think of breathing deep, that comes to me."

Anita: "That's perfect!"

John: "I see that as a portal into the spiritual realm."

Anita: "Yeah!

John: "That's like a comprehensive open portal to me."

Anita: "I didn't have the same experience, but for me, I breathed Bonnie (her leaving Earth physically immobilized me). I was breathing my love for Bonnie into every cell of my body. That was what I was doing."

John: "Yes, that's it!"

Anita: "I was filling myself up with that. Bonnie, her Spirit's Divine. The love that we carry for her, and she carries for us, is so powerful."

John: "Oh!

Anita: "So powerful!

John: "There's just a lot to it."

Grief is a gateway to the spiritual realm.

Anita: "It's more real. It's more real than being with the unconscious Earth person. You have the person, and you still have her consciousness. The body's gone; the enlightened consciousness remains."

John: "It's not just about Bonnie and us having this relationship. It's about what we do with it. It isn't happening just because we want to be with her or she wants to be with us. There's a bigger picture here."

Anita: "She brought me to the Grandmothers."

John: "Well, she's connecting us to everything of Spirit."

Anita: "Yeah!

John: "Yeah, right! When you meet somebody or when you're with somebody, you feel that and know that. That's one of the reasons why connecting with her allows us to connect more with others."

Anita: "That's true!"

Week 27: A Mother's Perception of Eternal Love

"There is no death, only a change of worlds"

—Chief Seattle

Guidance: Remember that the only death you experience is this earthly transition, a gentle passage from one form of existence to another.

In the vast tapestry of life, love is eternal—an infinite force that transcends all boundaries and time. It is the true essence of who you are, forever connecting you to everyone and to the Divine.

As you align your heart and spirit with the higher divine consciousness, you awaken to the beautiful truth that there is no true death. What you experience is transformation—an uplifting of your spirit as you draw closer to the source of love and light. In this

> *Love never dies.*
> *Love is eternal.*
> *The relationship*
> *is transformed.*

elevated state, you'll see that life is not an ending, but a cycle of renewal.

As you journey through this earthly realm, embrace the knowledge that you are a co-creator in the divine process. When you embody love and open yourself to the higher consciousness, you illuminate your own path and the paths of those around you. This sacred alignment gives you the strength to rise above the illusions of separation and fear.

Honor the eternal nature of love and the divine light that resides within you. Step forward with the courage and grace that I know you possess, knowing that you are forever connected and that your essence will never fade. In this profound truth, you will find peace, purpose, and the promise of everlasting life in love.

Breathe deep. Keep breathing.

Realization: In 2016, at age 65, I lost my 36-year-old daughter, Bonnie, in a car accident.

That's a whole story of magic, and I won't delve into it here, but after her passing, I felt like a tombstone—lifeless and heavy. My vitality and joy felt cremated along with her body, leaving me in a dark place.

During the initiation of grief, I experienced deep sorrow and isolation, struggling to find meaning and purpose in the aftermath of my loss. My "mother self" felt crushed.

In my sadness, I thought of Mary, who lost her son Jesus, and what that must have felt like for her. I also thought of Mother Earth and heard, "Now you know how I feel." It hit me like a jolt. It was time to shift my focus away from my sorrow.

Soon after, I received a message that there is no death. I instantly recognized this as truth. I understood that love is eternal. Searching for others who felt the same, I learned about the Forever Family Foundation and consulted with a medium on the first anniversary of Bonnie entering the Light. I discovered others sharing similar experiences.

I began to feel my daughter's presence despite her physical absence. In her presence, I felt a tinkling sensation, like the finest Koshi Aria chime flowing through me. My mind was filled with awe and wonder, and my heart felt as calm as gentle waves while I float in my kayak, soaking in the sun's warmth. Words cannot express the fullness of my experience; it can only be known through having the experience.

Initially, during the first 18 months after Bonnie left, I felt lost and unable to take action. Then, in December of 2017, I received a message from Bonnie urging me to start taking action. I began attending yoga, two mindfulness meditation courses, grief counseling, a grief group, Zumba, and gardening classes. I invited her into everything I was doing. I made an effort to set my grief aside in these activities, being fully present, knowing Bonnie was right by my side. When I focused on the moment, I could feel her presence, which reassured me that all was well. Things began to improve. My heart still carried deep sorrow, but I could venture out in public and mask it better.

In quiet moments, I would close my eyes and breathe deeply, allowing the essence of her presence to fill me. I understood I was feeling her presence—it was visceral. As a mother, I knew my child; that bond transcended the physical realm. In those moments, I realized that love does not cease; it transforms, becoming a guiding light that shines through the darkest times.

The love and the joy Bonnie brought me while she was on Earth is still present with me despite the absence of her Bonnie form. Now she shows up in forms such as trees, water, birds, animals, clouds, stars and people…

How Bonnie Shows Up:

Dreams: She shows up in my dreams.

Gifts from Nature: Feathers, heart rocks, fossils, trees, divine sunsets, moons, sunrises and cloud formations; She leaves me unique and unusual gifts from nature.

Signs or Symbols: She shows up as butterflies, hummingbirds and ladybugs.

Intuitive Feelings: I feel a strong sense of comfort being watched over and protected.

Unexplained Touches: I feel her hugging me.

Messages through Media: She leaves me messages through her old letters, cards, notes and songs on the radio.

Her Children: I feel her presence when I'm around her children, her siblings, and her close friends.

Memories: When I think of her, places where she lived, the things she loved, I feel her. Random memories pop up out of no where.

Increased Synchronicities: She lines things up to work things out. Things fall into place.

Nature Interactions: Unusual animal behavior, such as birds or butterflies approaching closely or following me indicate Bonnie is near.

Feeling Guided: Sometimes I feel guided by her.

Changes in Energy: When I feel her presence, I feel lighter or more peaceful.

Phone conversations: I purchased a princess phone specifically to talk to Bonnie. There's something special about the way we communicate through it. It's as though she's truly listening to my words. When I pause, I can sense her response in my mind. It's enough to reassure me that Bonnie is still with me.

In the things Bonnie loved: I often encounter her spirit when I engage in activities she was passionate about; such as art, creating, making salves, enjoying garlic, being in nature, camping, hiking, spending time at the beach or lake, thrift store shopping, and taking photos.

5 Keys to Knowing Love is Eternal

1. Love Transcends Physical Death.
2. Love is an Infinite Eternal Force.
3. Love Connects us to the Divine.
4. Love Transforms but does not End.
5. Love Empowers us to Rise above Fear and Separation.

Joyful Moments

- I visited with a friend. I listened to memories of long-ago jazz festivals and musicians. I love hearing people's stories.

- I realized I love to love others. It is my nature.

- Whenever I give love, it washes back to me in a wonderful full body feeling.

- I enjoy being listened to and telling my story without interruption.

- I kayaked this week, saw nature's beauty, and felt the wonder of the lake, the water, the trees, and the birds.

- I got into the cold water, and it was exhilarating.

- I had a fluid time at the hospice house—quite magical. We conversed about dogs and trees, which brought up the memory of the tree where he spread his wife's ashes. Then we sat in silence.

Journal

How do you embrace the no death mindset in your life? Have you lost a loved one? If so, how has that experience affected your perspective? Have you ever been hesitant to invite them in and feel their presence? What holds you back? Have you noticed signs of their presence? If so, what have you discovered? Reflect and answer these questions.

Joyful Moments: Reflect and freely write from your heart about your weekly joy experience or any insights you may have. Let your heart express itself through art.

Week 28: Grief

"We never lose our loved ones. They accompany us; they don't disappear from our lives.

We are merely in different rooms."

—Paulo Coelho

***Guidance:* Grief is the process of transitioning from having something to losing it.**

What you've lost can be returned; however, it will take on a different form. It is all up to you. Internal work is a necessary component of this process of transformation.

In this process, you acknowledge what was valuable and meaningful to you. Suppressing your sorrow can manifest in physical symptoms. While it may be tempting to avoid emotional pain, it is necessary to reconnect with it to move forward. Isolating or withdrawing from the pain can prolong the process of healing. Instead, face the pain head-on to find a resolution. Don't resist what you don't like.

Your belief system is ready for a shift. Recognize your feelings and emotions. Reset yourself by engaging in the present moment. Take some deep breaths so you can relax. Release attachment to what you have lost. Connect to your inner guidance. Allow your inner guidance to reframe your thinking. Now, your horizons have broadened. Your perspective has changed. Complete the process of dealing with pain from loss as it comes up. There is no closure with grief. Grief will change. You will grow from this experience. Things do get better—just another step in being a victor.

Realization: Grief is the gateway to the experience of God, a portal to the Light Spirit realm.

When one moves with Grief through the Creative Process, it accelerates the transformative process. Grief is the longing for the old relationship with that person . . . coming into a new relationship . . . ending the longing. We find ourselves in a higher vibratory frequency.

Grief is a misunderstood emotion that encompasses a range of experiences and processes. It is the yearning for something different, better, or more than what currently exists. It is a journey processed in the depths of the heart, and we find release as we navigate the intricate web of emotions and memories associated with loss.

Grieving Guidelines: No judging, no comparing, no apologies for human feelings, please don't stop the tears—it stops the process—feel it completely. No shortcuts.

When grieving, follow these specific guidelines for a compassionate and healing journey. Non-judgment and non-comparison are key. Remember that every individual's experience with grief is distinct and should not be compared to others. There is no need to apologize for experiencing human feelings, as grief is a natural response to loss.

Allowing the tears to flow freely; suppressing them can hinder the grieving process. By fully feeling and acknowledging the pain, we honor the depth of our emotions and permit ourselves to heal. There are no shortcuts in the grief journey; it is a process that requires time, patience, and self-compassion.

Our shared experiences highlight the transformative nature of grief. It is not merely about longing for the old relationship with the departed but rather about embracing a new relationship with our loved one in a different form. Through this process, we transcend the longing and find ourselves in a higher vibratory frequency connected to the Divine and the more extraordinary spiritual tapestry of life.

Indeed, grief becomes a gateway to the experience of God, a portal that opens the realm of Light and Spirit. As we move through the creative process of grieving, it accelerates our transformation, leading to a deeper understanding of ourselves and our connection to the spiritual realm. The longing for the old relationship gives way to a new, transcendent connection where our departed's presence is felt. We are victors.

Get back on the horse! In the scene from the movie *Gran Turismo*, the driver returned to the location of his accident and drove the course. Facing his pain and fear, a process, he went on to win races and become a champion.

Elements of Releasing Deep Grief

- Love was present.
- My emotional heart was engaged.
- A loving mother received me.
- I focused on memories of people who loved me dearly.
- I am surrounded by people who love me and don't judge me.
- I felt safe.
- Familiar with Grief, I knew what it was when she showed up, and I received her.

5 Keys to Heal from Grief

1. Embracing Grief as a Gateway.
2. Being a Victor, not a Victim.
3. Feeling the Grief Fully.
4. Recognizing the Shift in Identity.
5. Embracing Grief as a Friend.

Joyful Moments

- I realized that internal work is necessary for transformation.

- I was encouraged to face emotional pain head on for healing.

- My belief system shifted as I recognized my feelings and emotions.

- I connected to inner guidance and reframed my thinking.

- I now understand that grief is a gateway to the spiritual realm.

- I experienced joy and appreciation for my loved ones and joyful memories.

- I integrated and released long-held grief, resulting in feeling lighter and the rediscovery of a hidden self.

Journal

How has grief transformed your perspective and connection to the spiritual realm? Please reflect and answer the question.

Joy Moments: Write freely from your heart about your weekly joyful experiences or share any insights you may have. Allow your heart to express itself through art.

Week 29: Grieving is an Individual Journey

"Grieving is a necessary passage and a difficult transition to finally letting go of sorrow—it is not a permanent rest stop."

—Dodinsky

Guidance: No two people go through grief the same way.

Your way is not better or worse than anyone else. Give yourself all the time and space you need. Don't skip through any part of the process. There are no shortcuts. You choose to feel to heal. Love yourself. Seek comfort and support from those who will lift you up; pursue exercise, good nutrition, and guidance with which you resonate.

> *There are no shortcuts. You choose to feel to heal.*

Realization: Everyone has their own unique way to grieve.

Some process grief through the sweat of work using their bodies; instead of shedding tears from their eyes, they shed sweat through the pores of their skin. My husband did his grieving for our daughter as he sanded each log of our log home. It was done in silence and presence.

Shedding Tears

Everyone has feelings they express and process individually. However, the world tends to fail to acknowledge the grieving process of people who don't shed tears. It's not wrong or right. That's just who they are.

I want to acknowledge there are other ways to process grief that are just as valid as shedding tears. Just because we don't see men outwardly shedding tears the way women do, men can grieve and process through physical manual work. I didn't know this until I saw a grief counselor. Yes, we

> *Acknowledge there are other ways to process grief that are just as valid as shedding tears.*

all process grief differently. I just wanted to shed some light on it.

Yes, I agree. Tears heal the heart. My generation in the United States was modeled by our elders not to be "cry babies, be a man." Therefore, boys who stifled their tears later became men who could not express their tears or feelings. I am happy for people who don't have that programming. I, too, know those who have lost loved ones who needed to grieve but chose alcohol or drugs. Very sad indeed. Emotion is energy in motion. Grieve. It must be processed and moved out of the body through sweat or tears.

In my youth, I thought my parents' example was expressed truth. Unconsciously, I modeled that for my children. I am guilty of programming my son when I was unconscious . . . with "big boys don't cry." I have lived to know that it was wrong for me to teach that, and I have seen the suffering it has brought to men. I am sorry. *Ho'oponopono.*

5 Keys to Unlocking Grief

1. Acknowledging Different Ways of Processing Grief.
2. Challenging Gender Stereotypes.
3. Embracing Emotional Release.
4. Reflecting on Past Programming.
5. Seeking Forgiveness and Healing.

Moments of Aspects of Grief

- I listened to the sorrows of someone who feels disappointed. I have heard this story repeatedly, many times over many years. She called it lamenting. I was unable to stir up compassion.

- I felt irritated that someone thought they knew how I felt when they had never lost a child.

- There are many paths to the Divine. It is none of my business to persuade anyone.

- I love silence.

- I love peace and calm.

- I prefer dialogue as opposed to monologue.

- I love my life.

Journal

Reflect on any aspect of any grieving you have experienced.

Joy Moments: Reflect and free-write from your heart about your weekly joy experience or any insights you may have. Let your heart express itself through art.

Week 30: Do Not Skip Grief

"I have only slipped away into the next room."

—Henry Scott Holland

Guidance: **You have employed avoidance strategies, such as keeping yourself busy and putting on a happy mask to avoid facing your true emotions.**

However, these strategies have not allowed you to be authentic or address the grief and emptiness you were experiencing from a loss. The COVID-19 pandemic forced you to spend time with yourself and confront the unresolved grief within you, whether you wanted to or not.

Realization: Looking back, I realized I was afraid of nothing, emptiness.

I had to backtrack and let go of socializing classes and meaningless activities. I began to feel my emptiness. It turned out to be not as bad as my emotions perceived. Being alone, using art as therapy, being in the outdoors, exercising, gardening, meditation, connecting with nature, and practicing yoga helped me work with my grief. I found that my former identity was

I found that my former identity was gone. I was in the process of finding my new authentic self.

gone. I was in the process of finding my new authentic self. I could no longer tolerate the things I had previously overlooked, put up with, or stuffed. I was being made new.

Do not skip grief. Grieve fully.

Now, I know to feel my feelings as they come up. This is the hardest part for me. With help from my grief counselor, I recognize feelings, identify them, and express them using I-messages. I know my own needs and wants. Dealing with hardships correctly can elevate, give insight, increase love, and raise consciousness.

Look for opportunities in challenges faced. I am not a victim. If I don't think like a victim, I won't be a victim.

> *If I don't think like a victim, I won't be a victim.*

Grief Blesses Me

My cousin has a big heart and a capacity for love that matches it. When I am with her, I feel so loved. John and I spent three days with her and her husband at one of the Finger Lakes. I felt loved and received for who I am. We had so much fun just being together. Being with my cousin brought all the joyful family memories of my youth. My heart was whole.

Unbeknownst to me, things were lining up. We were at my cousin's home to tie up any loose ends for a family gathering the next day. The men were watching sports. On the dining room table were family photo albums of yesteryears. We were winding down from a day of preparing for our family reunion. It was a day of moving chairs, food shopping, rearranging the community room, and transferring food from the car to the room. It was a big day for me. My cousin graciously allowed me to pick the photos I wanted before the other cousins chose tomorrow.

It was about a half hour before others arrived. I tried to help my cousin in the kitchen, but I couldn't. I felt dizzy. I sat down . . . got out of the chair and felt dizzy. I was disoriented. It was a perfect storm—so perfect that my friend, Grief, made herself known. My heart quivered like Mercury as I received her. Tears flowed, and I wailed as deep feelings bubbled up and released.

I'm not sure what John thought was happening. I made sure he knew I wasn't having a heart attack. My cousin held me and walked me to her bedroom. She hugged me like a mother. It was a robust, energetic hug. I felt safe and encompassed. Waves of heartache, of loss released. Loss of my family, mother, and father, of my aunts, uncles . . . losses that I never attended to in my youth.

Now I feel lighter. My long-lost hidden self was integrated. Grief did that.

5 Keys to Not Skip Grief

1. Face your emotions.
2. Create space for grief.
3. Seek support.
4. Embrace change.
5. Practice self-compassion.

Joyful Moments

- I walked among the trees in the Tongass National Forest.
- I had lunch with John and my granddaughter.
- I had a phone visit with my daughter.
- I had a phone visit with my grandson.
- I walked in the rain.
- John and I spent the afternoon playing cards with our grand-daughter.
- I found a suitable raincoat for fishing in the rain.

Journal

How do your work with grief? Please reflect and answer the question.

Joyful Moments: Reflect and write free from your heart about your weekly joy experience or any insights you may have. Let your heart express itself through art.

Journal

Joyful moments: ...

PART 6

MEET THE FEELINGS
AND EMOTIONS

"The emotion that can break your heart is sometimes the very one that heals it."

—Nicholas Sparks

None of This Moves Me #1

John and I arrived at the Durango airport. Reaching for our IDs as we were ready for the security line, John realized he had left his wallet at home. Rather than me criticizing him or John berating himself, John calmly assessed the situation. Then, he drove back home to get his wallet.

When John returned, there was a long TSA line, and Pre-TSA was full. As we waited in line, the Pre-TSA kept filling up. Time was running out. We had five minutes before the gate closed. More people entered the Pre-TSA line as it was our turn to show our boarding pass and license.

I politely asked the lady about to have the next turn for the pre-TSA, "When do you board your flight?"

She answered, "7:20 a.m.".

I said, "Our flight departs at 7 a.m. Then I asked, "May we go before you?"

She graciously replied, "Yes, that's fine. I have plenty of time."

"Thank you so much!" I replied.

We buzzed through security. Then, an American Airlines worker came looking for us. Scooping us up, we left our electronic devices at the counter. Quickly, the American Airlines employees moved us through the gate. One of the attendants returned to Security to retrieve our left items. We were the last to board the plane. The attendant delivered our items to us. That was that! No real problem. No tizzy!

Handling the little things without emotional reaction or judgment trains you for significant life-changing events.

This just happened, so it is at the forefront of my thoughts. I can come up with plenty more examples, and I am sure you can think of your own. This is practice for the big one that throws you for a loop, like your daughter has a disability or a close family member has died. How does one maintain a semblance of order amid chaos? Handling the little things without emotional reaction or judgment trains you for a significant life-changing event.

None of This Moves Me #2

On October 20, John and I left at 8:00 a.m. to return home from a family visit in Oregon.

Last night, our flight from Phoenix to Durango was canceled; an unexpected overnight in a youthful hotel vibrating with energy and taxi rides followed.

We awoke at 4:00 a.m. this morning for a 7:30 a.m. flight to Durango. Getting to the airport at 5:00 a.m., we had ample time to go through Security and have a cup of coffee and muffin. Then, there was a mild delay due to a flight attendant's tardiness. The flight attendant arrived, and we all boarded the plane. Next, the small engine with the air conditioner didn't start, which caused more delay while the mechanic tried to fix it. It couldn't be fixed. The pilot deemed our plane unfit to fly. We all got off that plane, returned to a new gate, showed our boarding passes, and boarded another plane. That one worked. Off we went.

John and I arrived home safely in Durango at about noon. There were many opportunities to practice "none of this moves me." We came home safely. We were well treated, and we received vouchers—no big deal. We have much to be thankful for!

Week 31: Feelings Bring a Message

"Feelings are the language of the soul."

—Unknown

Guidance: Feelings are not just to be experienced. They are messengers guiding you towards deeper truths.

Listen to your heart. Embrace your unique way of moving in your world. Let your feelings guide you to authenticity. As you continue to heal, remember that every emotion carries lessons. By honoring your past and facing your grief, you create space for renewal and growth. Trust that as you

> *... feelings are meant to be dealt with when they arise. They are messengers bringing messages.*

connect with your feelings, you nurture your resilience and create a more fulfilling life. Allow yourself to feel fully, to breathe deeply and engage with the beauty and complexities of life, knowing that you are on a path to self-discovery and healing. Embrace this journey, for it is a testament to your strength and courage.

Realization: Today, I no longer suppress my feelings.

I never thought of myself as highly sensitive. When I was younger, I denied my sensitive desires. It took a toll on my spine, posture . . . I stuffed it. I love the idea of being an orchid. I always thought I was a dandelion because of my innate resiliency. I never really considered my feelings or that I even had them.

Finally, being retired, with time to do my inner work, I have released my stuffed feelings. The truth is I retired after my daughter passed, and I could not stuff down my grief. I did try, but my body turned into a concrete block. I was a walking gravestone. I literally could not walk. The pain was unbearable. I went to my physician, and when the assistant asked me how I was doing, I broke down in wailing tears. He asked me if I wanted to see the counselor. I told him, "No! My body is the problem." I met with the physician, and he referred me to the orthopedic doctor and physical therapist.

With the orthopedic appointment came a series of tests. The results showed usual aging but nothing that should cause this rigid body experience. I went to the orthopedics physical therapy associates, which was like a warehouse experience. After six weeks, I still had the same problems.

While working out in the whirlpool at my local recreation center, I met up with an old teacher colleague who had lost her son ten years earlier. She highly recommended a physical therapist (PT) she went to who did trauma work.

I started with this recommended physical therapist. He had been trained in trauma work, so this is where we started. I lay on the floor, and with knees bent and feet on the floor, I shook my body for 20 minutes. I did this daily at home until no more shaking occurred, based on a study of mammals who automatically shake after an injury. I saw my PT regularly, and my body responded to his physical therapy practice.

We had all these looming issues . . . related to our daughter's sons. It was clear. I could not keep and raise them. My body could not do it. No matter how much I wanted to, raising Bonnie's two sons was not mine to do.

I needed help. I started asking Bonnie for help. I got an internal message from her that she had a plan and would guide John, and me.

I went to a grief counselor and bared my soul to her. She helped me identify my grief. Together, we identified and named my emotions. She demonstrated several ways to express them. She explained that by not listening to my feelings, I was inwardly stuffing them as pent-up emotions. Lying dormant, these emotions were triggered by feelings happening in the now. It would show up as an overreaction to what was said or done.

She advised me to meet each feeling and find out what memory was attached to it. She taught me to communicate my feelings using I-Messages: I feel—— when you . . . as I think.

What Are "I" Messages? Dr. Haim Ginott came up with the idea of "I" messages. This technique helps us express our concerns with more understanding and non-confrontationally, which can lead to a positive response from the other person.

Life has taught me to listen to my feelings and adjust to offer something to my world, my work. I accept my sensitivities, allowing myself the pleasure of indulging my sensitivities: being alone, connecting with nature, doing one thing at a time, enjoying beauty, listening to music, dancing, appreciating and understanding the cycles of life, relaxing, loving, holding, softening, feeling, trusting, knowing, profoundly breathing, enjoying the wonders of life. I no longer stuff my feelings.

I no longer need to accommodate, or please; I can feel it all. My spine and muscles are unwinding. I am healing myself. True resiliency comes from facing, meeting, and communicating feelings. No more pushing through and ignoring my feelings! It took me sixty-six years before I realized this self-imposed health hazard.

5 Keys to How Feelings Bring a Message

1. Body pain.

2. The body can become rigid, and experience physical limitations.

3. Address emotional trauma.

4. Feelings are messengers with messages: Feelings are meant to be dealt with when they arise. Identify and name emotions and understand the memories attached to them.

5. Using "I" messages to communicate feelings.

Messages that Brought Joyful Moments

- Finally releasing stuffed feelings after retirement and the passing of a loved one.

- Meeting a physical therapist who specializes in trauma work and finding relief through their therapy practice.

- Acknowledging and accepting that raising Bonnie's two sons was not my responsibility.

- Seeking guidance from the departed loved one and receiving an internal message that they have a plan.

- Seeking help from a grief counselor and learning to identify and express emotions in a healthy way.

- Learning and practicing using "I" messages to communicate feelings effectively.

- Embracing my sensitivities and indulging in activities that bring joy and pleasure, such as being alone, connecting with nature, and enjoying beauty.

Journal

How do you process your feelings? Reflect on your feelings. Are you in tune with them? Clarify and write about your feelings.

Joy Moments: Reflect and free-write from your heart about your weekly joy experience or any insights you may have. Let your heart express itself through art.

Week 32: Feelings and Emotions

"Feelings are as valid as facts, and emotions are the key to connecting with ourselves and others."

—Brené Brown

Guidance: **Within each of us, there exists a duality of emotions, light and shadow.**

Just as the ancient Cherokee tale speaks of two wolves fighting within, you each have an internal struggle between the wolf of love, joy, and compassion, and the wolf of anger, fear, and resentment. The key, as the old Cherokee told his grandson, is that the wolf that grows strongest is the one you choose to feed.

You go in the direction of our focus. What you feed grows. There is a duality of emotions, and you don't need to judge them as bad or good, but you do need to feel

Emotions are energy in motion. Let them move. They are not meant to get stuck in your body.

them and let them move through your body. You breathe into them. Emotions are energy in motion. Let them move. They are not meant to get stuck in your body. They were never intended to be acted upon. They were meant to be felt and loved, and in that way, they keep moving and out of you into the light.

Do not dwell on sorrowful, fearful, worried, or angry feelings. You work to clarify the realm of the heart and mind. You do it for yourself. This internal work opens the channels to allow joy to flow. Remember, "Been there, done that, learned the lesson," and act accordingly.

At first, on the path of joy, all kinds of suffering, pain, and heart-ache show up; observe and witness them. Then, listen to feelings, messages, and insights. How can it be seen from a higher perspective? How can these insights bring light to your unconscious mind? The light goes on, "Aha!" As soon as any darkness that is not yours or that you have already dealt with comes up, you send love to it.

Stay away from side trails. You can get lost. Feel it and let it go. Turn your focus to the direction you want to go. Give it all to Light. Get back on your path to joy. You found your way out. Joy! You are not your emotions or your feelings. Your feelings give you insight into your internal state.

However, there are also emotions that don't move through us so easily. These are the ones that tend to get stuck, hang around, and become attached to our minds. This is where the real work comes in - unraveling the thoughts and beliefs that are keeping those emotions from flowing freely.

Realization: We all have our way of meeting our emotions.

Both the ones that move through us and the ones that linger. This is my practice: Remember to breathe into the lower belly when an emotion or feeling presents itself. Breathe slowly and steadily. Stay in the here and now. Observe without judgment. Who is observing? Identify as the observer.

I am not my emotions; I am the observer of my feelings. Breathe. Identify the emotion. It fits into one of these three major categories: happy, sad, or mad. Think of it as a tangled ball of yarn that needs to be unraveled. What thought triggered the emotion? Change the thought. Did the emotion change? I keep changing my thoughts until I feel good in my body.

Another approach is to focus on the feeling in my body. I am not my feelings. I am the observer of my feelings. How does my body feel? Where do I feel it? Tight? Loose? Hard? Soft? Pain? Relaxed? Throbbing? Pulsations? Go to the one speaking the loudest. Breathe into that part of the body. Be curious. Wonder. Ask, 'What do you want to tell me?' Listen.

If I have time, I go to the next body part that needs attention—breathing into it. I repeat the previous process. Listen. Note what that feeling needs. Do I need to let something go? See it differently? Do it differently? Change my perspective? Is there a truth I need to realize?

Through this process of hearing and listening to my body, particularly the left iliotibial band tract or IT band (ITB), I learned what changes I needed to make in my habits. I made the changes. I am in the process of healing. I am moving better and feeling.

5 Keys to Being the Observer of Emotions and Feelings

1. Mindful Awareness.
2. Non-Judgmental Observation.
3. Identify as the Observer.
4. Unravel the Thoughts and Triggers.
5. Listen to the Wisdom of Your Body.

Strategies for coping with negative feelings:

- Slow my breathing

- Breathe in Light and Love

- Notice nature. Pay attention to colors, hues, shapes, textures, temperatures, movement . . .

- Think of someone I love

- What am I feeling? What thought created the negative feeling?

- Release the feeling

- Give thanks

- Be kind to someone

Joyful Moments of Feelings and Emotions

- After two months of intense body strength training to return to Zumba and kayaking, I went to Zumba. I hadn't been in nineteen months, and my performance improved. My training worked! I felt delight, joy, and satisfaction.

- After nineteen months of not kayaking, I thought I would never kayak again, but I went kayaking at Lake Nighthorse. I felt great joy!

- I have released my dear loved one who is struggling. I have done all I can. I felt frustrated because I was trying to get her to change. It is out of my control. It is all up to her. I told her she was not alone and that I was there for her. She has another perspective. It is no longer mine to do. The ball's in her court. I love her from a distance. She must do her work. It is her journey. I am not to meddle.

- I appeared publicly and spoke. I felt confident as I spoke my truth and was happy with the outcome.

- I led a peace ceremony. I felt nervous about how it would fit in with the hostess's plan. Working with it in the present moment, it all fell into place. The energy was potent.

- In a small group, I met a 45-year-old European woman who conquered the same struggles that a loved one in the US has. She brought me hope with the possibility of overcoming the anxiety one is born with. Anxiety became her teacher. Joy bubbled up, and tears of joy came to my eyes.

- I felt apprehensive about meeting this new person, but that feeling did not stop me. I made a heart connection with the person. We had so much to share on all levels, and joy bubbled up.

Journal

How did feelings and emotions speak to you this week? Reflect and answer the question in your journal at the end of each day.

Joyful Moments: Reflect and free-write from your heart about your weekly joy experience or any insight you may have. Let your heart express itself through art.

Week 33: None of This Moves Me

"None of these things move me."

—St. Paul (Acts 20:24)

Guidance: You have control over what you say and how you respond.

As you navigate this journey, recognize the power of observation and the clarity it brings. So, choose to embrace the creative process of Life, let internal pressure build, and contain it. By doing so, you tap into a wellspring of strength and resilience that propels you forward. You are not your emotions. You are not your feelings. You are not your mind. Be the observer. Stay in inner peace. Allow your destiny to come forth.

Realization: My experience in living has taught me not to judge or label these changes as good or bad. Instead, I practice accepting and acknowledging them as they are.

To steward the creative process in my realm of responsibility, I practice not reacting impulsively to these changes. Life has taught me that what is present in my life is part of the ongoing creative process.

Although it seems counterintuitive to the human mind and emotions, receiving things, as they are, creates forward movement. When I have a non-judgmental attitude toward the changes and developments in the world, I can observe and appreciate the creative process unfolding. Yes, I feel it. I maintain my center. My branches bend like a tree when the wind blows, but I don't get uprooted. I come back to being grounded in the truth of myself.

Keeping a clear perspective allows me to see beyond biases and programming, fostering a sense of openness and wonder so something new can appear. In this way, I can make rational decisions. It took me a long time to learn and trust that this process is how to handle things. It allows me to step back, viewing circumstances from the "mountaintop," which gives perspective. In turn, I grow and learn. Rather than react in haste or want things to be different than they are, I can respond thoughtfully and adapt to the evolving nature of the world around me. It is what it is.

"You get what you get, and don't throw a fit!" These were words I often used as a parent and teacher. What is the point of "None of this moves me? Something remarkable happens when I refuse to react or be moved by negativity. I find myself no longer being triggered or controlled by it. For example, for travel delays and flight cancellations, rather than getting distraught, I actively focus on the present moment, witness what is happening, identify any feeling, breathe through it, and continue paying attention to my breathing and surroundings. I am letting things work without judging or labeling them. I've discovered the path of joy—a way to move through life's ups and downs with a sense of empowerment and resilience.

I can contain the internal pressure it creates by not allowing negativity to affect me. Instead of letting it consume me or dictate my emotions, I harness its energy to propel my life forward. It's a powerful force for change that keeps me in the present moment, alert to what is coming down from heaven, to let manifest what Life has intended for me.

When our daughter Bonnie passed, John and I felt it, but we decided not to take it as the worst thing in the world but viewed it as an opportunity to handle death differently. That turned out to be a major blessing to us. Here's another example: when we decided where our grandsons would live, we waited to see what Life presented to us rather than letting our minds ruminate on a solution. Life offered a better "solution" than we could have imagined. Everything showed up just as we needed it. We acted when we needed to act. It was not always easy. Life supported us.

This journey of not being moved by negativity has become an integral part of my creative process. It has taught me the art of letting go and maintaining inner peace and stability. By consciously choosing not to be swayed by external factors, I become the architect of my emotional well-being. I am no longer at the mercy of circumstances; I am the creator of my reality. But let me clarify, not being moved by negativity does not mean denying or suppressing my emotions.

> *By consciously choosing not to be swayed by external factors, I become the architect of my emotional well-being.*

On the contrary, it's about acknowledging and processing them healthily and constructively. I understand that emotions are a natural part of the human experience, and I honor them. However, I decide how much power they hold over me. It's about finding a delicate balance between resilience and emotional authenticity.

As I walk this path of joy and refuse to be controlled by negativity, I'm discovering the immense potential within myself. The possibility of being who I came to Earth to be. I found my creativity in art, gardening, writing, cooking, teaching, and all my creative pursuits. I developed the power to shape my life, to create the reality I desire, and to radiate positivity to all those around me. It's a transformative journey that aligns my actions and intentions, allowing me to live a fulfilling and purposeful life.

5 Keys to None of this Moves Me

1. Acceptance and non-judgment.
2. Present Moment Awareness.
3. Emotional Resilience.
4. Letting Go.
5. Creative Expression.

Joyful Moments

- Observing John handle the dilemma of leaving his wallet at home. Instead of reacting negatively, he calmly assessed the situation and drove back home to get his wallet.

- I politely asked the lady in the Pre-TSA line if I could go before her because my flight was departing earlier, and she graciously agreed; it shows the power of kindness and empathy.

- Despite the flight delays, cancellations, and plane changes, we maintained a positive attitude and practiced "none of this moves me."

- I was grateful for the safety of our travels, the kindness of others, and the blessings in our life.

- We had a long wait at the Belize airport. January 1 is a big travel day.

- Once we arrived in Belize, everything seemed to fall into place.

- We took time in solitude, feeling grateful we were in one place for three weeks.

Journal

How do you stay centered and calm when something triggers a response? Reflect and answer the question in your journal at the end of each day.

Joyful Moments: Reflect and free-write from your heart about your weekly joy experience or any insights you may have. Let your heart express itself through art.

Week 34: Inner Guidance

"Our inner guidance comes to us through our feelings and body wisdom first."

—Christiane Northrup

Guidance: **Start acting from your highest vision. Love yourself.**

Find your Joy—no more sorrowful thoughts. Still your mind, pay attention to your breath and listen for the still, small voice within. You are in the process of awakening to your higher consciousness. You learn to differentiate between inner guidance and ego. Feel it. How does it make you feel? Icky, headache, sick to your stomach? That's ego. A feeling of peace and well-being? That's inner guidance. Your experience is exclusive to you. Ask your body how it feels. The body will tell the truth.

> *Ask your body how it feels. The body will tell the truth.*

Listen to inner guidance. It is the voice of love and truth. This is your inner guidance who connects you with All That Is. It is a momentary practice. You retrain the mind to enjoy the present moment. The more you listen to your inner guidance, the more your mind comes to trust it. Eventually, you become one with it.

You are in a process of clarifying your consciousness. Unconscious cultural programming keeps you bound. It comes down to this: You are being called to your Divine Nature, to live in the highest frequency of Love and Light. It is not about joining a group. It's about your incarnation as a Divine being on Earth.

Tools and Practices for Opening to Inner Guidance

✓ *Meditation:* Regularly meditating can help calm the mind and make room for your inner stillness. Find a quiet spot, sit comfortably, focus on your breathing, and let your thoughts flow without judging them.

✓ *Journaling:* Writing out what's on your mind, how you feel, and your experiences can help you figure things out and connect with your gut instincts. Find some quiet time to write in a journal and let your thoughts spill onto the page.

✓ *Mindfulness:* Focus on the present moment and be aware of your thoughts, feelings, and body sensations. Practicing mindfulness can help you better understand yourself.

✓ *Intuition exercises:* Don't forget to focus on activities that can help you build and rely on your intuition. For instance, you can pay attention to your instincts when making decisions.

✓ *Nature connection:* Take some time to enjoy nature and soak in its beauty and peacefulness. Being in nature can help you feel grounded and connected to your inner guidance.

✓ *Seek silence and solitude:* Create some quiet time for yourself every day. By disconnecting from distractions and finding moments of peace, you can experience your inner peace.

Connecting with your inner guidance is a customized journey for everyone, and what may be effective for me might be different for you. I have used tools such as the I Ching, muscle testing, the pendulum, angel cards, inspirational books, and sighting animals.

5 Keys to Inner Guidance

1. Start acting from your highest vision.

2. Love yourself.

3. Find your joy.

4. Be still and listen.

5. Trust your feelings.

Journal

How can you incorporate the keys to inner guidance into your life? Reflect and answer this question in your journal.

Joyful Moments: Reflect and write freely from your heart about your weekly joy experience or any insight you may have. Let your heart express itself through art.

Week 35: Inner Beauty

"To be beautiful means to be yourself. You don't need to be accepted by others.

You need to accept yourself."

—Thich Nhat Hanh

Guidance: **You are enough, worthy, and beautiful.**

Love yourself, accept all of it with love, and be your authentic self. Shedding the light on what's beautiful, don't be fooled. Beauty is an inside job. It has nothing to do with eye color, nose size, skin color, hair color or texture, body size, height, or age. Beauty is the radiance within shining through one's body . . . the inner peace, pure heart, clear mind, and higher consciousness. Think for yourself. Stop acting from the conditioning of commercialism and marketing. You have been duped.

Advertising makes the unconscious believe they are not pretty, not the right size or shape, or good enough. Wake up! You have been programmed to buy stuff. The media has convinced the dominant culture that you are not enough just as you are. You are enough. You are worthy. You are beautiful. Love yourself, accept all of it with love, and be your authentic self.

Inner beauty encompasses the qualities, values, and attributes within a person's heart and soul. It goes beyond physical appearance, manifesting through thoughts, actions, and interactions with others. Kindness, compassion, authenticity, resilience, empathy, gratitude, and love are all aspects of inner beauty that radiate as a genuine and uplifting presence.

Popular culture defines beauty by superficial attributes such as eye color, nose size, skin color, hair color or texture, body size, height, or age. Contrary to the dominant cultural beliefs, inner beauty is rooted in a loving heart and the genuine ability to love oneself and others. Inner beauty is about aligning oneself with truth, pure love, and the qualities that define true character. One taps into one's inherent power when one connects with and expresses this inner beauty.

True beauty emanates from within, encompassing inner peace, a pure heart, a clear mind, and a higher consciousness. It does not conform to societal standards or succumb to the conditioning of commercialism and marketing. Marketing and advertising have deceived you into believing that you need to be more pretty, that you are not the right size or shape, or not good enough as you are. It is time to wake up and question why you are buying into these illusions.

Remember, you are more than enough, worthy, and beautiful. Embrace and accept all aspects of who you are with love. Let your authentic self shine. Know that you are as good as anyone else. No one is better than you. Stand tall and be proud of who you are. Do not feel ashamed of your body, body parts, or looks. No two people are alike. Look at nature's diversity; like the flowers blooming from the same seeds. This is the way things are meant to be.

Realization: I am incredibly grateful for my daughters and daughter-in-law, who have opened my eyes to the harmful impact of body shaming.

It is genuinely demeaning and unjust. The dominant culture in which I was raised promoted a consciousness of modesty, shame, guilt, and the evils of the flesh. My experiences of life made this incongruent with my understanding. Along with enculturation, when I was a teenager, I got catcalls for my big breasts, which caused me to slump, cover, minimize, and want to be invisible. It took me many years to correct my posture. I am no longer ashamed of my breasts. I stand tall and proud and walk like the queen I am. I must constantly remind myself to put my shoulders up and down and reset my posture. I often wish correct posture was taught in grade school as a mandatory class to attend until one mastered good posture.

5 Keys to Inner Beauty

1. Embrace Your Qualities.
2. Love Yourself and Others.
3. Reject Societal Standards.
4. Stand Tall and Proud.
5. Let Your Authentic Self Shine.

Moments of Inner Beauty

- Enjoying the early morning stillness of the western horizon.
- Holding a space of love and non-judgment when someone is feeling hard times.
- Having meaningful conversations with Conversation Dinner friends.
- Initiating the steps to get strength training for summer kayaking.
- Creativity allows me to see things in a new light.
- I am feeling deep gratitude for my spouse and the support and encouragement he gives me.
- Courage to speak up and lead when it is mine to do.

Journal

When did you experience inner beauty this week? Reflect and answer.

Joyful Moments: Reflect and free-write from your heart about your weekly joy experience or any insights you may have. Let your heart express itself through art.

Week 36: Fear

"Always do what you are afraid to do."

—Ralph Waldo Emerson

Guidance: Take time to consider the fears you wish to release.

List them on a piece of paper. Prioritize them. Pick the one with the highest priority to work on.

Realization: I overcome fear by reminding myself that I am on a healing journey.

My inner guidance reveals the truth of/for myself and expresses my authentic voice. Nothing can stop me until my work is complete. I feel an energy inside and around me that is holding and protecting me. It reminds me that fear is nothing but a messenger. The more I meet, face, and do the things I fear, the more confidence and assurance I feel. The fear dissipates.

Release Fear Process and Meditation: Embody a Fearless Life

You can ask your inner guidance questions like: What message is fear bringing to me? What is fear keeping me from? Or you can choose your own questions. In the past, fear taught me to be better prepared, think things through before acting or saying "yes," be proactive, spend more time relaxing, and listen to my body.

You'll need some paper to write and a pen. (Do not confuse fear with caution.) Below, I have listed some common internal fears.

- Fear of revealing your imperfections
- Fear of not being liked or loved
- Fear of being different
- Fear of being ostracized
- Fear of being called weird or crazy
- Fear of the unknown
- Fear of not fitting in
- Fear of not being good enough
- Fear of being made fun of
- Fear of being judged
- Fear of failure or success
- Fear of domination or control
- Fear of being alone
- Fear of facing fear
- Fear of death
- Fear of emptiness or nothing
- Fear, fear, fear . . . the list is endless

Below is the meditation to release fear. The intention is to release fear and be unencumbered. Take your time. Let your heart guide you. Feel each word.

Trust whatever fear comes up for you is just the right one. See it as an opportunity to face fear, and let fear dissipate. Are you ready to begin releasing your fear? If not, stop here. If yes, proceed. You will start the process of fear release and becoming unencumbered.

Get comfortable, sitting upright with two feet flat or lying flat on the floor. Breathe normally. Now, take four deep, slow breaths: inhaling, holding, exhaling, and pausing for the count of four. Silence. Focus on your heart. Still your mind. Breathe Love in. Pause, Relax, and Feel. Bring your intention to your mind. Pause, Relax, and Feel. You now are ready to let go of your fear.

- Name the high priority fear you want to release here (refer to your list if necessary).

- Be with your fear. Acknowledge your fear. You are safe.

- Feel your fear. Where do you feel fear in your body? When does this fear show up? What triggers it? Observe your reaction to it. Change in heart rate? Flush of heat? Tightness in your body? Where does the tightness or tingling show up in your body?

- Together with your fear, do Ho'oponopono. "I am sorry for not addressing you when you first made an appearance. Please forgive me for stuffing you down. Thank you for holding this feeling until I was ready to face it. I love you. Together, we say: We are sorry. Please forgive us. We thank you. We love you."

- What have you learned from living with this fear? Write down what you have learned.

- Thank fear.

- You are now ready to let fear go. Love your fear messenger.

- Fear is a feeling messenger. It has brought you to this moment. You are now ready to listen and face fear. Write down the message. Pause and relax as long as needed.

- Fear has done its job. You can say goodbye and let it go. Freeing up energy that held fear is a relief.

Love expands the Heart. Pause, Relax, and Feel. Love opens the Heart. Pause and relax. Feel your Heart open. Love is Wise. Pause and relax. Feel your Heart's Wisdom. You are Love. Pause and relax. Feel. You are loved. Pause, Relax, and Feel. Love gives and receives Blessings. Pause, Relax, and Feel. Be Still and listen to the Silence. Pause, Relax, and Feel. Be Peace. Pause, Relax, and Feel. Feel the Courageous Spirit that you are. Feel at a visceral level the Adventurous

Spirit that you are. Feel the strength of your Heart. Feel the wonder of the Universe! The wonder of the Cosmos! The wonder of yourself that is waiting to be revealed.

Now take the fear list, tear it up, dispose of it, or file it away and return to it sometime in the future, your choice.

5 Keys to Being Free of Fear

1. Trust! Everything is Working Out for Your Highest Good.

2. Pause, Relax, and Feel.

3. Listen to What Your Heart Wisdom tells you.

4. Expressing Your Authentic Self.

5. Enjoy the journey.

Journal

Remember, you are a steward of this process of embodying a fearless life. Catch yourself when fear shows up. What feeling message is it giving you? Remember not to take it back. Fear is nothing. Return to your Love. Follow your Heart. Write about your internal experience during and after this fear-release process.

Repeat this meditation as often as you like. If fear persists and keeps you from progressing, seek a trained professional or medical attention.

Joyful Moments: Reflect and free-write from your heart about your weekly joy experience or any insights you may have. Let your heart express itself through art.

Week 37: Worry

"Worry never robs tomorrow of its sorrow. It only saps today of its joy."

—Leo Buscaglia

Guidance: **You can no longer ignore the message worry sends you.**

Constant worry is a waste of time and energy. Worry signals a problem, so address it and take care of it. Be done with it! A worrier creates worries by not taking the time to listen to the worry message. Anxiety becomes a crippler in one's life. The worrier walks around sad, looking for agreement, creating more sadness and misery. Why would anyone want to do that?

It is better to find out what message worry has for you. Listen thoroughly to worry. Could you write it down?

1. Address the message.
2. Look at the problem.
3. Create a plan.
4. Put the plan into action.
5. Take the first step in the plan. Pick the most straightforward step to do first.
6. Do what is yours to do.
7. Execute and complete your plan.

If the problem persists after you have done all that was within your control, you know it is out of your control. You need to accept that "it is what it is." Whatever is out of your control, please give it to the Divine.

Trust the Divine. All things are unfolding in Divine Timing. It is no longer yours. Know the Divine is taking care of it. As things unfold, you see what yours is to do. Do that. Do not take the control away from the Divine. At this point, it would be very foolish to think you can do it better than the Divine. You would be back to where you started.

Realization: To take it back by worrying, I see as insulting the Creator.

How could I think I know more than the Creator when, in fact, I don't? Do not judge. Let the process work. (Would I look inside a mother's womb at four months and consider the gestation process good or bad? No, I would not, because I am smart enough to know it is incomplete.) Let the Creative Process work!

If the thought or feeling of worry returns to my mind, I wrap it in Divine Love and Light. I don't take it back. I don't entangle with it. I offer it peace. Lifting it in my consciousness, my heart radiates love and light. I return it to the Creator. This process is transmutation.

I remind myself that this problem is not mine. My Higher Power is directing this creative process. It is not mine to judge. Now, I am free to be happy and enjoy life.

Important Note: The Divine is directing this Creative Process. It is not mine to judge. Things may get worse before they get better. Hold steady and let the pressure build. This pressure is needed for change to occur. (Recall how the steam engine or pressure cooker works.) Let the Creative Process work. Judging releases the pressure and may even abort the process. Thus, the process will need to be reinitiated.

5 Keys to Stop Worrying

1. Identify the underlying source of the worry.
2. Address the message.
3. Analyze the problem.

4. Create a plan.

5. Take the first step of your plan.

Moments of Joy Beyond Worry

- Finding peace in addressing worries.

- Discovering self-awareness through reflection.

- Being empowered through problem-solving.

- Feeling accomplishment through taking action.

- Trusting in the Divine timing.

- Letting go of control and judgment.

- Feeling happy and enjoying life.

Journal

How can you free yourself from worry and have a worry-free mind and a happy, blessed life? Reflect and answer this question.

Joyful Moments: Reflect and write freely from your heart about your weekly joy experience or any insights you may have. Let your heart express itself through art.

Week 38: Love Heals a Broken Heart

"Healing is an art. It takes time. It takes practice. It takes love."

—Unknown

Guidance: The breath is love.

All the answers to the Universe are within you. You are your guru. There are no mysteries. Go within, breathe in, and breathe out. Be conscious of your breath.

In the breath, there is no fear. Fear takes you out of the reality of oneness with the Universe. Body, mind, and spirit were designed to work in sync. The breath informs the heart, the gut, and the mind. When the breath is shallow and fast, you enter a state of heightened anxiety. When it is slow and deep, you experience presence and peace.

For a happy life where you are fully functioning, you need to breathe in the Star chakra energy, a massive disk of light above your head. It provides you with an ever-flowing energy. It has your name on it. It is yours. You choose to invite it in. Breathe it in, deep into the root chakra.

Allow the breath to spiral around your trunk, spiraling through your sacral chakra vertically upwards so every block opens and the energy flows unhindered. This should get the whole system flowing and vibrating.

Now, move to your solar plexus and do the same thing. Repeat breathing into your heart, next to your throat, then your third eye, and your crown. Feel it in your whole being. This is who you are and who you came to be. Your breath makes you whole. You are Divine. Express from your place of being. Then, your expression is Divine.

Keep your spine straight. The spine is the complete channel through which the Universe's focused healing and intelligence flow.

The respiratory system is the conduit. The breath ignites every system: circulatory, digestive, respiratory, endocrine, excretory, and nervous, including every organ, muscle, bone, tissue, and DNA in every cell in your body.

Realization: My world came back to life, a new world, more beautiful than I had before.

My meaning returned. I saw everything with new eyes. I could see and feel Love and Light in everything. Nature had a new meaning to me. I connected in Love with the elements, the trees, and Mother Earth.

I returned to the things I had always loved and learned new things. I danced, sang, gardened, swam, kayaked, hiked, and healed. I reconnected with my inner core, heart and its beat, and my breath. And so, it continues in effortless effort.

5 Keys Steps to Heal a Broken Heart

1. Breathe consciously.
2. Access the Star chakra energy.
3. Unblock and flow: Focus on each chakra, starting with the root chakra and moving through the sacral region, solar plexus, heart, throat, third eye, and crown.
4. Embrace your Divine nature.
5. Maintain good posture.

Moments of Joy from Healing a Broken Heart

- Realizing the power of breath.
- Feeling the ever-flowing energy of the Star chakra into my being.
- Feeling the relief from the blockages opening up and movement of the life force through me.
- Feeling my Divine nature.

- As I keep my spine straight, I realize the Universe's healing and intelligence are moving in me.

- Knowing the breath nourishes every system, organ, and cell in my body.

- I allow my expression to come from my inner guidance.

Journal

How can you heal your broken heart in your daily life to support the wholeness of your heart? Reflect and answer this question.

Joyful Moments: Reflect and write freely from your heart about your weekly joy experience or any insights you may have. Let your heart express itself through art.

Week 39: Change

"Once you make a decision, the universe conspires to make it happen."

—Ralph Waldo Emerson

Guidance: You always have a choice.

You are free to choose your behavior and your attitude. You might not always know it, but you understand how this works when you become a conscious adult. You can be like the stuck needle of an old record player saying things, saying the same old stuff, repeating the same old behaviors, and having the same experience every day, over and over again, for thirty or more years.

Nothing changes—same miserable outlook. Everywhere you go, you get persecuted. Everybody hates you. Everybody is mean to you. Nothing is fair. Everybody gets all the breaks. You get nothing. You get angry. You punish yourself. You ingest the things that take you further away from reality. It doesn't have to be this way. You have a choice. A choice of what you say, think, and do every moment. Your choices create your reality.

How does one fix a stuck vinyl record arm? First, you recognize it. Then, you lift the arm and remove the dust from the needle. Then, you gently place the needle back on the record turntable. Check to see if the record is playing a new song. Listen, let it play. If it gets stuck again, check the record for dust. Clean the record. Do what it takes to clean it thoroughly. You choose to do the work yourself; no one else can do the work for you. Return the record to its position on the record player.

Look at the needle again. Remove all dust from it. Now, turn the record player on. It should work fine now. If not, replace the needle.

You replaced the needle. Is it still stuck? Maybe there is a scratch. Check for a scratch. If so, every time the same old song repeats itself, lift the arm carefully and place it where there is no scratch. Does it keep getting stuck? Time for a new record.

What song do you want to hear? What story do you want to tell? It is your choice.

Realization: I want an inner song and story that creates happiness.

A life that reflects that; sorrows come and go, but there is always a happy ending. On my path of joy, in which I listen to my heart's desire, I follow the joy breadcrumbs I find along my path. The singing breadcrumbs led me to take Hospice volunteer training. Unsuspecting, it plopped it right into my lap. I have been in hospice training for the last two days.

A dear friend told me all about starting a "Threshold Choir." I was immediately interested, seeing it as an opportunity to sing. I longed to sing with a small group with a purpose. I sang in grade and high school every Sunday at church, weekly choir practices, and state and national competitions. Enthusiastically, I said, "Yes!" I created a playlist on Spotify entitled "Threshold Choir Anita Albright."

I was told I needed to become trained as a hospice volunteer to participate in a hospice choir. Naively, I thought, "Sure." In 1993, after the death of my brother John, I inquired about being a hospice volunteer. At the time, I was not ready. I am now training to be a hospice volunteer.

Before I left this morning for Day 1 hospice volunteer training, I consulted Bonnie's Angel Cards, created by Doreen Virtue. My question: What is my time at hospice training about? I selected the "New Love" card. My assumption is my new partner is my hospice patient.

At the close of the first day of training, I realized the choir was not for me to do. A new door is opening to me. Being a hospice volunteer with no agenda may just be what I need to do.

On Day 1 of hospice volunteer training, I learned that a hospice volunteer sits and offers presence and calm to hospice patients. Be present and be peaceful. The volunteer documents any changes. Three volunteer hours a week. I am good at being present and actively listening.

My vulnerable self is afraid. I have been through death and grief—the grief of the loss of my daughter. My body feels worried that I will plunge into despair. I need clarity. I ask the Divine, "What would you have me do?" I always get this message back: "Be."

Spirit works with me this way: Spirit plops it in my lap. It always comes through an unexpected door. A total surprise! Everything flows effortlessly with no blocks. The only thing that blocks me is my need for clarity. With that, I do my internal work.

Day 1 Guidance: Follow your inner guidance. Be yourself, be present, and let it be. You are held in the arms of the Divine. You are so loved. Why are you being called to sit with the dying? Does your decision align with your heart's desires? Engage in practices that help you connect with your inner wisdom. To

Trust in your journey and be patient with yourself.

gain clarity, it can be helpful to seek advice from trusted mentors, spiritual leaders, or experienced individuals. Consider volunteering in a hospice setting on a trial basis. It's like trying on a coat; you can put it back on the rack if it does not fit. You will have a firsthand experience of what it's like to be in that environment and to engage in the activities. See what you resonate with. Pay attention to how you feel during and after these experiences. Do they bring you a sense of fulfillment, peace, and purpose?

Remember, clarity may not come all at once. It may unfold over time as you self-reflect, seek guidance, and take steps toward exploring your calling. Trust in your journey and be patient with yourself as you navigate this process.

Through text with a brief explanation of why I wanted to see her, I set up an appointment with my grief counselor for Day 4. My grief counselor texted me, "A gentle reminder the universe goes with you wherever you go, trusting your wise heart to guide you. I think you would be a phenomenal hospice volunteer. You walk with very little fear, but the system you have to participate in . . . is fear . . . if that makes sense, that's probably what you're picking up in your primal sensations."

Day 2: Today starts the second day of the training. I am two-thirds on board to be a hospice volunteer. The other third of me, my two lower chakras, are confused and fearful. I fear falling into some abyss of grief over Bonnie when I know otherwise.

On day 2 of the training, the door opened wider. We had an activity in which we experienced the loss and grief of what the dying patient was going through. I was okay with it. Grief did not slice me down. We also had a dyad activity in which, with a partner, we listened to our partner tell the story of the last time we saw our loved one who died. As listeners, we should not reflect or think of what we would say next. We each had five minutes to speak and five minutes to listen. I told the story of the last time I saw Bonnie. I had never told that story to anyone. I was calm and present throughout the entire process.

Day 2 Guidance: As a hospice volunteer, bringing your presence and calm to a dying person for three hours can have several benefits for everyone involved. Your presence can comfort and support the dying person during their final moments. Your calm demeanor and compassionate presence can help alleviate their anxiety and provide peace. Spending time with a dying person allows you to establish a meaningful connection with them. Your presence and active listening can give them a feeling of safety and being heard.

Your presence can also benefit the family and loved ones of the dying person. Knowing their loved one is not alone and having someone caring for them can give them relief and comfort. Volunteering in hospice care can be an enriching experience. It can provide an opportunity for personal growth, compassion, and reflection. By bringing your presence and calm to a dying person, you contribute to the community's overall well-being.

On Day 3, I filled out the required hospice volunteer forms.

On Day 4, I met with my Grief Counselor to get her insight. I am clear in myself. "Trust myself" and know that what shows up, I can meet with serenity. My fear has dissipated. I returned my completed, signed Hospice volunteer packet to the HV coordinator's secretary. I passed the background check and drug test. Thus begins my journey as a hospice volunteer.

Two months later . . . I want to quit.

Five months later . . . I am all in.

Nine months later, I took off my Hospice volunteer coat. While the experience was gratifying and meaningful, the role ultimately did not fit my lifestyle. After each visit, I found my energy depleted. Listening intently for three hours as a hearing-impaired individual was quite exhausting. Following each volunteer session, a significant rest and recovery time was required. My body spoke to me and I listened. I stepped aside from Hospice volunteering.

5 Keys to Making a Decision that Brings Joy

1. Reflect on your intentions.

2. Seek inner guidance.

3. Seek external guidance.

4. Test the waters.

5. Trust the journey.

Joyful Moments in Decision-Making

- I have a choice. This realization brought a sense of joy and freedom.

- I took action to change my circumstances, which gave me hope and possibility.

- Embracing new opportunities: Discovering the possibility of becoming a hospice volunteer gives joyful moments of decision-making.

- Seeking guidance and support for decision-making brought clarity and reassurance.

- Testing the waters by volunteering in a hospice setting on a trial basis, I experienced firsthand the fulfillment, peace, and purpose of being present for others during their final moments.

- Trusting my process, I eventually found clarity by being patient. I felt trust and peace.

- Be open to change. One thing leads to another.

Journal

Reflect on one of the decisions you made recently. Write about your decision making process.

Joyful Moments: Reflect and write freely from your heart about your weekly joy experience or any insights you may have. Express your heart through art.

Week 40: Let Go of Judgment

"Judging a person does not define who they are. It defines who you are."

—Unknown

Guidance: Stop judging.

Judging something as good or evil can knock you out of your inner peace. The new generation is losing the structures of the older generation. It feels different and awkward. Welcome it! The old paradigms are shifting. Don't judge it as good or bad. It is what it is. It's sort of like no expectations . . . no judgment. You do what you do without concern for results.

Some human beings remember their inner peace. As they express this peace, their actions make all things new.

Stop telling people what to do. Let people find their way and solve their problems. Mind your own business. You are not here to change anyone's mind or convince anyone.

No hurry. Everything is working out in its perfect time.

Realization: My job is to enjoy what is right in front of me.

Non-judgment is a powerful and transformative mindset. I have stopped classifying what I see as good or bad. It simply is. I know that the sun always shines, regardless of any temporary clouds. My attitude affects the outcome. I possess the power to change my attitude. Non-judgment allows me to maintain control over my words and responses. My energy is directed toward creating and transforming. I am confident that my thoughts shape my reality and that happiness is an inside job. Through non-judgment, I can cultivate a state of well-being in my mind and body.

5 Keys to Help You Stop Judging

1. Embrace the present moment.
2. Embrace change.
3. Cultivate inner peace.
4. Respect individual autonomy.
5. Embrace patience.

Joyful Moments Without Judgment

*   Viewing the summer sunset.
*   Getting photos of the sunset.
*   Creating a one-minute YouTube video from my photos of the sunset.
*   Being all packed and ready to go on a weeklong trip.
*   Getting a phone call from a dear friend.
*   Nurturing my body when I feel sick.
*   Talking on the phone to Sabina.

Journal

How can you let go of judgment and embrace a mindset of acceptance and non-interference to experience inner peace and allow life's natural rhythm to unfold? Please reflect and answer the question.

Joyful Moments: Reflect and write freely from your heart about your weekly joy experience or write about any insights you may have. Let your heart express itself through art.

PART 7

GRATITUDE

"Stormy or sunny days, glorious or lonely nights, I maintain an attitude of gratitude. If I insist on being pessimistic, there is always tomorrow. Today I am blessed."

—Maya Angelou

Finding Gratitude in Every Turn

While we were in Belize, climbing the Cahal Pech Maya ruins reminded me that my 72-year-old body needs to stretch daily, get up, move, and limit my sitting time. Never stop learning!

As John and I were walking, we took a left up a hilly road that went straight up. As we passed the first house, a Maya grandmother called us from her porch. She told us we were going the wrong way, pointed us back to where we made our turn and followed the road. I am thankful for that grandmother. That intervention made the rest of the walk to Cahal Pech lighter.

There are plenty of stairs to climb at Cahal Pech. The temperature was 94 degrees. Luckily for us, cloud cover appeared and cooled things off. I was hot, sticky, and sweaty.

On the walk home, we were ready for a cold beer. Walking by the San Ignacio Casino, we saw the sign "Bar." We headed inside. Greeted by a friendly security guard, we told him we wanted a cold beer. He took our backpacks and locked them in the cabinet.

Then, the lady clerk wrote down the information on our driver's licenses and took a photo of us. Going through all this for a cold beer seemed like a big deal.

The place was air-conditioned. After walking through the casino, we went to the bar and ordered two cold beers. The lady bartender said, "No cold beer." We weren't interested in a warm beer, so we left, determined to find a cold one.

The security guard was surprised that there was no cold beer. We all laughed. The bouncer directed us to the San Ignacio Resort, just next door. We headed over and ordered two Landsharks. He gave us each an icy mug.

We sat outside on comfy lawn chairs, enjoying the shade, cool tropical breeze, and two ice-cold beers. We were thankful for this outcome!

Memories of the Joys of Water

When I was growing up, my family would go to the ocean. After my parents left, I stayed for a second week with neighborhood friends who were also spending a second week.

I had a good friend whose whole family spent time at the ocean. Her mother had been my fifth-grade teacher, whom I respected, so she knew I behaved mannerly. I had the best time with that family.

Throughout the year, my mom signed me up for swimming lessons. I was a good swimmer but would have needed more strength to be a lifeguard.

When I was at the ocean, I spent every day swimming in it, riding the waves, diving under the waves, floating on my back, relaxing, listening to the water, and watching the sky. That is heaven to me.

I love deep, fresh water to swim in. My mom loved to swim, too. My father didn't, so swimming was something I did with my mother. Swimming at the quarry pool was a daily event for us during the summer. As I became more independent, my friends and I would go without parental supervision. We'd walk two miles to the pool. We never had a problem walking. No one ever bothered us on that walk.

There are several ways to enjoy the quarry, which has been transformed into a swimming hole. I loved swimming in the deep fresh water and diving into its depths. One of my favorite ways to do so was the "Pulley Rope Jump." Several other modes of entering the water include the Tarzan swing, pier, cliff diving, three levels of diving boards, and two steel water slides: one on the deep side and a shorter one in the shallows. A concrete wall separates the shallow water from the deep side. A sandy beach is adjacent to the shallow water.

The Quarry Swim Pool also has a pavilion. There was a canteen where they sold snacks and beverages, a jukebox, and a dance floor. The music was current rock & roll. After swimming, we danced. Under the Pavilion, they had a teenage dance every Friday and I went every Friday night. I love to dance.

I can list all the large bodies of water I have swam in the Atlantic

Ocean, Pacific Ocean, Caribbean Sea, Honduras Sea, Chesapeake Bay, Mediterranean, Tyrrhenian, Ionian Sea, Lake Powell, Sea of Cortez. I love water!

Summer Adventures

In 1973, John and I spent the summer camping across the United States. We drove our 1962 VW Bug and ventured into the unknown. Every day was a new adventure. Gas was twenty-eight cents a gallon. We stayed in national and state parks. We slept in a pup tent and cooked on a Coleman stove.

Eventually, we skipped the tent set-up and slept out under the stars. We only spent one night in a motel in Estes Park, after we were flooded out by rain on the Middle Saint Vrain River.

Our 1973 Summer Travels

- We started on I-40 and headed south to the Great Smoky Mountains.

- There, we started driving back roads and seeing what we could see.

- We crossed the Ozark Mountains in Arkansas.

- We camped along a creek. This was my first experience hearing coyotes.

- We crossed the Mississippi River on a ferry.

- That was the first time I experienced people making eye contact, smiling, saying hello, and giving you the time of day, an experience I loved and wanted more of. It turned out everyone we met was like that.

- We visited every small town we came to. The people in small towns were friendly.

- The outdoors and nature were friendly, too.

- We meandered out West.

- We spent three weeks in Colorado.

- Camped in Yellowstone, Washington, Oregon, California, Dakotas, Texas.

Six years later, in 1979, we moved from Baltimore, Maryland, to Durango, Colorado. After over forty-five years, we still live in Durango and love it.

My Grandmother

My mother always talked lovingly about her parents and siblings. My mother only had good things to say. I know only a little about my grandparents. They were upright pillars in their community and contributing members of their church. My grandfather was a construction and plumbing foreman. He owned his own house. Grandpa was literate. He helped others fill out documents. He ran a tight ship. Everything was clean, neat, and in order. Grandma's meals were homemade. I remember Grandma. Grandpa died when I was two.

My grandma was in her late teens when she came to the United States with Grandpa. Grandpa was much older than her. Never returning to her homeland, Grandma never saw her mother again. She raised her six children—three boys and three girls—with love, respect, and discipline. All her children were talented, artistic, musical, athletic, intelligent, mechanical, and hard-working. My grandparents valued education. Grandma was devoted to Blessed Mother. Grandma loved to sing, dance, and cook. She made all her children's clothes. After all her children left home, sewing in a clothing factory filled her days. Her children loved her and cared for her as she aged.

The first saddest day of my life was when Grandma passed away. I was in the third grade. She died from diabetes. Grandma never left me. She is forever in my heart. (The first poem I ever wrote was about her.)

Early on, I felt a special bond with her. I know she loved being with her children and grandchildren, although, I only saw her on holidays. We traveled nine hours in the car to Rochester to visit our extended family. I remember playing hide and seek in her house, a handmade handkerchief jumping mouse, eating homemade popcorn she made on the stove, spaghetti drying folded over the back of a ladderback chair, and playing card games. I remember her smile, her laughter, and her singing. I wanted to be like her: full of love and happiness.

Whether or not you knew your grandma, everyone knows the spirit of the grandmother. Here are some things I know about my grandma.

- Grandma loves you just as you are.

- Grandma loves you across time and space.

- Grandma loves you forever.

- Grandma always welcomes you. She loves it when you come and visit her.

- Grandma loves having fun. She likes to play games, especially the ones that you like.

- Grandma never judges you.

- Grandma believes in you.

- Grandma is always encouraging.

- Grandma will help you in any way she can.

- Grandma wants to see you happy.

- Grandma has the magic to lighten everything up.

- Grandma understands what you're going through. You are part of her. You are never alone.

- Grandma only sees the good in you and what you are doing right.

- Grandma wants to be with you all the time, but sometimes Grandma gets tired and needs time to rest.

- When Grandma corrects you, she's sweet about it.

- Grandma can be funny.

- Grandma may need your help, too. Ask her.

- Grandma likes to see you love your brothers and sisters.

- Grandma likes to see you respect your mom and dad.

- Grandma likes to see you doing your work and helping at home.

- Grandma likes to see you take care of what is yours to do.

- Grandma likes to see you caring for yourself.

- Grandma wants you to have fun and enjoy life.

- Grandma wants you to blossom and grow. Discover and develop your talents.

- Grandma wants you to avoid bad influences and self-destructive behavior.

- Most of all, Grandma wants you to know what real love is and that you are always loved forever by Grandma.

- At the age of eighteen, what you make of your life is all up to you. Do not blame your parents or your DNA.

- Remember this: You play the hand you are dealt to the best of your ability.

- Turn to Grandma; she is always there for you. Just call on her. Invite her in.

How I Met the Grandmothers

I had been following my life's path, but something was missing. I was doing inner work. I followed Bonnie's guidance to heal from her June 20, 2016, passing.

Because of Bonnie's love of nature, I always felt she was Mother Earth's daughter. Looking out of our south window at the trees, our hundred dead pinyon trees came to mind. Mother Earth said, "Now you know how I feel." My perspective changed. I started seeing and connecting with nature, the trees, the flowers, and the plants in a whole new way. I was feeling their spirit.

In January 2018, a friend interested in plants in Zumba class told me about a gardening class through the county extension service. I applied for it. The application required an essay on why I wanted to take the class. My response was honest: to learn more about Mother Earth. I took this graduate-level Colorado Master Gardener class. Re-engaging in learning was like a life preserver that pulled me back to shore. It was the resuscitation I needed after a drowning.

I was feeling like parts of myself were returning with this new awareness for gardening: the soil, the climates, the insects, the PH balance, the microorganisms, plants, trees, wildlife, and temperatures, I completed the class. In April 2018, I became a Colorado master gardener volunteer, working the community gardens, the botanical garden tours, and the information county extension booth at the Farmer's Market. I was feeling whole again. Along with that, I grew some vegetables in my garden. I also harvested lavender and made salves.

In July 2018, John, Sabina, and I spent three weeks traveling throughout the Italian island region of Sicily. It was a trip we were going to do with Bonnie. It felt like she was with us. There, we visited the villages of my grandfather and grandmother. I felt my roots, my blood, my heritage: Mediterranean, Ulysses, the history, the Greeks, the Romans, the Arabs, the Normans, the welcome, the hospitality, the spirit of the people, the land, the climate, the warmth, the music, the food, eggplant, pasta, tomatoes, the wine, the chocolate, the olive oil, Mount Etna, solar panels, windmills, farm to table, the craftsmanship, and the bodies of water. I was home. That experience rooted me and gave me a sense of belonging to the ages.

I didn't know I was being primed for the Grandmothers. In retrospect, I was. In November 2018, I pushed myself to go to a birthday party. There I saw some old and dear friends. One of them officiated Bonnie's Celebration of Life. Her son and Bonnie were childhood friends.

In our thirties, my friend and I spiritually grew up together. She mentioned a Grandmothers' circle she was doing at Heartwood co-housing every Thursday morning and invited me to join. I declined because I did Zumba on Thursdays, and I couldn't miss it. Then she suggested I read a Grandmothers' book. She thought I'd like it because I was 'Yin.' I trusted her and purchased *A Call to Power: The Grandmothers Speak, Book 1* by Sharon McErlane.

After reading that book, I quickly read Sharon McErlane's other two Grandmothers' books. I resonated with the Grandmothers' message. I already knew the concept of the Net of Light through working with the Attunement which is the radiant current of Divine Love and Light. I resonated with the spirit of the Grandmothers. I

> *The Grandmothers deepened my understanding of Divinity by including the Divine Feminine and Mother Earth.*

knew I was here to embody my divinity. The Grandmothers have shown me an easy way to do it. The Grandmothers deepened my understanding of Divinity by including the Divine Feminine and Mother Earth. It made sense to me that Bonnie was guiding me.

I moved through the many aspects of grief from my daughter Bonnie's death and found joy, beauty, and power. I knew Bonnie guided me to the Grandmothers.

In December 2018, I contacted the Net of Light (netoflight.org) about the Grandmothers. I received a welcoming letter from them. Then, I received an email from a local grandmother inviting me to one of Durango's Net of Light meetings. It took me two months, but I got there.

In March of 2019, I attended my first Grandmothers' Circle. The magic was that I felt entirely at home among these women. Okay, you need to know, I had no idea what I was getting myself into. I went into the kitchen. We were sharing food, and everybody was friendly. It was like these people already knew me.

Then we sat in the Grandmothers Circle, and I don't remember how it all went, but I do remember that we went around the circle introducing ourselves. Then something extraordinary happened. I found out that each person there had a connection with one of my family members. Their child had a connection with Bonnie, or they had a connection with Mary Ellen, John's sister who is deceased. Later, I discovered that one of the grandmothers even had a daughter who was friends with my son, John. She set up John with Emily, who is now his wife.

With COVID-19, I joined the Net of Light meetings on Zoom, which are still held worldwide. It's been a fantastic way for me to connect with my grandmother sisters from around the globe.

Inside, I was growing and changing. I'm sorry to say that I could not relate to my old friends like I used to before Bonnie died. I tried hard to make it happen, but this big void existed. I had become a different person after Bonnie's death. My focus had shifted, and I realized the preciousness of my time. I was aware that I needed to use it wisely. I couldn't explain why this change was happening to me, but I had to honor what was emerging within me. I had so much of myself to explore. I had to do it alone.

I began painting. I took some painting classes. What was coming from my art was a revelation of my subconscious. I saw the process I was going through internally. I was blossoming. It was an amazing internal journey, and I was on it. I realized I had been keeping myself busy to avoid the feeling of nothingness.

I had a week to myself while John went to Lake Powell with his buddies. It was during this time that I met the Great Nothingness. I found it was nothing to fear. I saw in the nothingness a beautiful experience full of love and life. I finally could relax, and I no longer had to do it. I had to be.

> *Net of Light is the ever-present Light within and in everything.*

My experience of being in the void led me to be all-in with the Net of Light and the Grandmothers. I followed what I was called to do. I knew what to do. When I got out of the way, things were effortless. I appreciated working with the Net of Light. I could see the difference it was making reflected in my world.

As I reflect on the Net of Light that has come together on Earth, called forth by the Grandmothers, I am reminded of the connections we share. When we speak of "the Grandmothers," we refer to the Divine Presence that reveals itself when invited into our lives. This invitation extends to all forms of the Divine—God, Jesus, Mary, Higher Power, Creator, Quan Yin, Angels, Saints, Ancestors of Light, Divine Light, and Unconditional Divine Love. The Net of Light is inclusive, embracing all races, genders, and belief systems, allowing each person to embark on their unique journey with the Divine. In this shared space of love and acceptance, we find not only solace but also the strength to heal and grow together, united in our quest for understanding and connection.

Week 41: Steward of the Earth

"The Earth does not belong to us; we belong to the Earth."

—Chief Si'ahl Seattle, Suquamish Leader

Guidance: Your world changes when you change your consciousness (removing root disbeliefs rooted in separation from the truth, which has created the false reality).

This is how you know heaven on earth. It happens in consciousness first. You are a steward of your planet. Connect with her every day. Thank and love the air that breathes everything. You are one.

Realization: I thank and love the earth of my body, the land I live and walk on, all I see, and nature.

I commune with Mother Earth as I honor, listen to, and hear her messages. As I listen and follow her guidance, a creative process follows. I act when I feel called to act. I speak when I feel called to speak. I become a walking blessing on Mother Earth.

This joy journey has led me to mindful meditation, yoga, Zumba, the Colorado Master Gardener CSU course, amending my soil, composting, community gardens, working at the farmers' market, growing herb, vegetable, and flower gardens, creating herbal salves, the Celtic medicine wheel, connecting with my ancestors, the Grandmothers, Yin Yang balance, the Net of Light, Ancestors of Light, photography, art, singing, communing with the elements of air, water, earth, fire, and ether, trees, birds, deer, insects, joy, stillness, silence, volunteering for the Net of Light earthly organization, the Energy Ball Peace Ceremony, the board of ARC, and the 7 Days of Rest Event. I am inspired to keep listening to my inner guidance. I ask, "What is mine to do?" My best work is done in the vibratory field.

Some people like cars, technology, books, toys, food, fashion, and gadgets. I like those things, too. I love things from nature: the natural expression of nature, its cycles, rhythms, changes, balance, movements, sounds, tastes, and smells; elements, the water, the wind, the air, the earth, fire; trees, plants, flowers, animals; the planets, the stars, the cosmos, and life itself.

I love being in nature. I marvel at its beauty and wonders, and I love its diversity. This love comes from deep within me. Being with nature grounds me. I have found that spending time alone with nature gives me peace and sustains me.

- Seeing nature mistreated, I feel sad.

- Seeing plastics rolling in on the ocean waves, I feel sad.

- Seeing trash along the beach, I feel sad.

- Seeing people disrespect nature, I feel sad.

- Seeing the mistreatment of animals, I feel disgusted.

- Seeing the misuse of nature, I feel sad.

- Seeing the earth's resources misused, I feel sad.

- Hearing of children being shot and killed, I feel enraged.

- Hearing of child abuse, I feel fiery.

- Hearing of hate crimes, I feel anger.

- Hearing of poverty, I feel injustice.

- Hearing of greed, I feel injustice.

- Hearing of lies, I feel furious.

- Becoming aware of hidden agendas, I feel manipulated.

- Hearing of rape, bullying, predatory and dominating behaviors towards anyone and anything, especially the weak and innocent, I feel rage and violation.

All the above makes me feel very sick in my stomach. It is not mine to absorb. I give it to Mother Earth. I am getting in touch with my feelings. I am new to feeling my feelings and am working on expanding my range of feelings. It is all rudimentary; I have limited experience in identifying my feelings. (Bear with me.)

Rather than stuffing or acting out my feelings, I prefer to own and feel them and change my behavior or thinking. I look at nature for insight. My answer lies in my human expression of integrity, truth, kindness, care, and respect for all living things (including myself) and their diversity. That should keep me busy.

5 Keys to Being a Steward of the Earth

1. Connect with and appreciate nature.

2. Listen and follow nature's guidance.

3. Engage in eco-centered practices.

4. Advocate for the Earth.

5. Strive to live with integrity and kindness towards all living things.

Moments of Gratitude

- Connecting with and thanking the Earth and the air I breathe.

- Communing with and honoring Nature.

- Engaging in mindful meditation, yoga, and Zumba.

- Participating in gardening and working at the farmers' market.

- Creating herbal salves and exploring Celtic medicine.

- Connecting with ancestors and the elements of nature.

- Volunteering for environmental organizations and participating in peace ceremonies.

Journal

How can you deepen your connection with nature and embody gratitude in your daily life to become a steward of the Earth? Please reflect
and answer the question.

Joyful Moments: Reflect and freely write from your heart about
your weekly joy experience or any insights you may have. Let your
heart express itself through art.

Week 42: The Joys of Water

*"Let yourself be silently drawn by the stronger pull of what
you love.*

*In the depths, there is a spring with all the water your heart
is thirsty for."*

—Rumi

Guidance: Stay active and take breaks from sitting for too long.

Do not hesitate to ask for help and be open to new ideas and solutions.
Find happiness in the little things and cherish the present. Pursue
your passions and hobbies because they bring you joy and fulfillment.

Realization: I Love Water.

I love waterfalls, rivers, creeks, springs and ponds. I love hot springs
and saunas, too. I love flash-freezing water and seeing images in it. I
love walking in the rain and splashing in puddles. I like playing in the

snow too. I like showers and baths. So, I get it. Water is my thing. I am a water lover. Water is my muse.

5 Keys to the Joys of Water

1. Connection with nature

2. Childhood memories

3. Variety of water experiences

4. Appreciation for water in all its forms

5. Personal connection to water

Moments of Joy with Water

- Kayaked at the lake.

- Swam in the lake.

- Drinking an ice-cold glass of water on a hot, dry day.

- A tub of warm water for washing the dishes.

- Rain! Glorious rain that makes my garden grow.

- Water in our drip irrigation system that waters our garden while we are traveling.

- Recently, I attended a four-hour lecture by Veda Austin. Water resonates with frequency, energy, and vibration, revealing its connection with everything.

Journal

How has water shaped and influenced your life, both physically and emotionally? Please reflect and answer the question.

Joyful Moments: Reflect and write freely from your heart about your weekly joy experience or write about any insights you may have. Let your heart express itself through art.

Week 43: Gratitude: Life's Gifts and Finding Joy in Every Moment

"Give thanks in all things."

—George Shears

Guidance: There is a Creative Process. You are on Earth to be a steward of it.

If you allow whatever it is "to be without judgment," you will be blessed and held through your whole process, not dissipating substance by losing your center. Feel it and be thankful for life's gift, even if you don't see it or like it. The gift is hidden, and you will find it. Just stay present. I know this to be true: joy will eventually be the outcome.

Realization: My mother trained me to be polite early in life.

Saying "thank you" was taught to me as an essential response to something given or done for me. Mom drilled it into me and my siblings. For this, I am forever grateful. (Thank you, Mom.)

In the last seven years, I found that "being thankful for what is" yields joy.

Everything that comes into my life may not have the appearance of a gift, but I receive it as a gift and welcome it. I have a thankful heart.

. . . everything that comes into my life may not have the appearance of a gift, but I receive it as a gift and welcome it.

I see everything as a gift, even the death or disease of a loved one. The moment it comes, I welcome it. I give thanks for it. I hold steady. It seems counterintuitive, but it's not. It takes reprogramming, changing thinking, and automatic responding from "what is" is disastrous, awful, the worst to a welcoming attitude. It took sixty-six years of practice to get this. It works!

Once I got it, nothing moved me off my center. I feel it. I get the message from the feeling. I listen to the message. I reflect. Receiving "what is" in this way empowers, increasing inner strength. It's like filling up the gas tank. Things lighten and lift.

5 Keys to Gratitude

1. Training in Politeness.
2. Welcoming "What Is".
3. Being Thankful for "What Is".
4. Seeing Everything as a Gift.
5. Practice and Inner Strength.

Journal

How can gratitude transform your perspective and bring joy into your life? Reflect and answer the question in your journal at the end of each day.

Joyful Moments: Reflect and write freely from your heart about your weekly joy experiences or write about any insights you may have. Let your heart express itself through art.

Week 44: Gifts from Grandma

"Grandmother. The true power behind the power."

—Lisa Birnbach

Guidance: **You may call your grandmother Grandma, Nana, Mimi, Oma, Nona, or Abuela.**

It doesn't matter what you call her. Everyone knows the feeling of their grandmother. It's all the same spirit. Whether or not you knew your grandmother, it doesn't matter. Think sweetness, kindness, wisdom, and playfulness.

Realization: **My connection to my grandmothers, grandfathers, and other ancestors comes to me consciously or unconsciously.**

I feel their loving support when I participate in their customs, interests, hobbies, habits, qualities, talents, and capabilities. My extended family strengthens me through the ages in whatever I do. I choose to let go of their traditions that no longer serve me. My mother always spoke lovingly of her parents. I know only a little about my grandparents, but I carry their legacy within me.

My mother played an important role in shaping my interests and values. It was through her that I was exposed to yoga, hiking, swimming, exercise, gardening, community service and a commitment to living according to principles. From my early age, she modeled the value of quiet reflection, active listening and engaging with the natural world. She was intelligent and independent, a loving wife and mother. My mother instilled in me the importance of pursuing my career and developing myself beyond a wife and mother. She respected all people, regardless of their color, nationality or religion. She was mature, wise, patient and kind. I so appreciate the loving guidance and understanding she provided. She was a loving grandmother to my children.

Whether or not you knew your grandmother, everyone knows the spirit of the grandmother.

5 Keys to Connecting with the Spirit of Your Grandmothers

1. Love and Acceptance.
2. Bonding and Support.
3. Fun and Playfulness.
4. Growth and Development.
5. Connection and Belonging.

Journal

How have your grandmothers influenced you? Please reflect and answer the question.

Joyful Moments: Reflect and freely write from your heart about your weekly joy experiences or any insights you may have. Let your heart express itself through art.

Week 45: Be the Rock

"When one makes the mind stick to one thought, the mind becomes rock-steady and the energy is conserved."

—Ramana Maharshi

Guidance: **The characteristics of rock are strength, stability, resilience, and solid.**

Rocks can be immovable, steadfast, unchanging, unwavering, grounded, dependable, reliable, and withstand adversity.

Realization: **Living on Earth has its ups and downs at every level in every location.**

I am not getting on that roller coaster ride. I need to be in position to be a rock in my world. I am practicing the internal exercise of returning "to the rock-steady state inside me," so I am ready when something big comes with feelings that may trip me up. When I notice the off feeling, rather than going down that rabbit hole or getting sucked in being off center, I automatically return "to the rock-steady state inside me" rock energy.

The Plan

Step 1. I must know how I feel when I am rock-steady and unmoved. I get familiar with that feeling and ground myself in it. I feel that and know that.

Step 2. I know how I feel when I am off-center. I think of something that pulls me off my center. I feel that. I am familiar with that. Now I have two baselines: for rock and off-center.

Step 3. Now, I am ready to begin my practice of returning "to the rock-steady state inside me." Think of something that takes me off-center; I feel it. Now, I go to my rock-steady state. I feel that. I anchor myself to that. One practice completed.

Step 4. I commit. I practice this exercise often until it becomes automatic. Like any exercise, I do, I will improve with practice. It is on my daily "to do." My goal is mastery.

This is a good practice for me in these shifting times.

5 Keys to Being a Rock in Your World

1. Know Your Steady State.
2. Recognize Off-Center Feelings.
3. Practice Returning to Your Steady State.
4. Commit to Regular Practice.
5. Embrace Shifting Times.

Joy Moments of Being the Rock

- I observe quietly without saying a word.
- I refrained from lecturing and teaching.
- I felt my vibrational energy.
- I am at home in my inner garden.
- I appreciated the beauty of our summer garden.
- I am employing 20-second hugs and six-second kisses with my spouse.
- I am feeling deep gratitude for the presence of John in my life.

Journal

How do you cultivate and experience strength and stability within yourself amidst the ups and downs of life? Please reflect and answer the question.

Joyful Moments: Record your joyful moments. Let your heart express itself through art.

PART 8

LEARN FROM THE BODY

"When we're awake to our bodies and senses, the world comes alive. Wisdom, creativity, and love are discovered as we relax and awaken through our bodies."

—Tara Brach

An Ideal Day in Belize

John and I spent the night at the Maya Bella Hotel in San Ignacio, Belize. It's a great in-town location! We walked everywhere, including Cahal Pech Mayan Ruins, which was an exertion for me. (This is an excellent reminder to keep doing Zumba and yoga.)

We wanted to beat the heat, so we got in the car early the following day. On the drive to Xunantunich, we bought homemade ham, cheese, and jalapeno burritos from two local lady street vendors. That breakfast was just right. We arrived at 7:10 a.m. at Xunantunich Mayan Ruins, which allowed us to find a tour guide and be first in line for the ferry.

My right hip was hurting, so using a walking stick might help relieve the pressure. (My walk to Cahal Pech told me I needed help to climb, possibly a cane, which I didn't have. I planned to go as far as possible, then sit in the shade.) Being extra early, I got talking to one of the Mayan vendors, Cannell. He told me I must see the view from the top of the pyramid. He connected us with his cousin, a tour guide. I asked Cannell if he had a cane for sale. He didn't. I decided to see if there were any sticks under the trees. Cannell smiled, stopped me, and showed me the handle he unscrewed from the broom. I was lucky that he shared his broom handle with me. I am so thankful! I was able to use it as a cane. The broom handle assisted me greatly in climbing to the top of the El Castillo. By the way, the ferry that crosses the river into the ruins operates for tours from 8:00 a.m. to 4:00 p.m. The time at the ruins took about two and a half hours.

With care, we could climb to the top of El Castillo—130 feet tall—the second tallest building in Belize. We highly recommend a tour guide. Ours made the site come alive for us. Gersch was conscious of our aging bodies and kept a pace that suited us. We gained knowledge and understanding of this ancient Mayan culture, its rise and downfall, and their knowledge of astronomy and nature. I am very thankful to have visited Xunantunich. I studied the Mayan culture in college and was fascinated by it. I now know why.

Getting off the ferry, I returned the broom handle. I visited with Cannell, learned about him and his family, and bought some of his items. Then, I met Gersch's mom and made an excellent connection. Hara and I had a lot in common.

Week 46: Healing My Nervous System

"Nature does not hurry, yet everything is accomplished."

—Lao Tzu

Guidance: **Earth is going through a cleansing process. It makes sense that your Earth body is cleansing, too.**

Your entire life, you've been wanting to slow down. Somewhere in your nervous system, there is this component or belief that you don't have enough time, that you must hurry up and speak fast because there's not enough time for people to listen. People will start talking over you, so you talk fast to get it all in. That is not good for your nervous system. Your entire life, you have been unwinding this tangled pattern.

Realization: **Life is teaching me to slow down and do what is mine to do.**

I am learning to be at peace with what is. Life is teaching and guiding me.

It is no longer my job to multi-task. Instead, I have chosen a slower pace. I am doing one thing at a time, being present, fully engaged in the moment. When I find myself hurrying, I stop what I am doing. Take a break. Engage in something that leads me to a balanced pace. This pace comes from a place of peace within.

I have found that place both internally and externally. I call it Bliss, a place of home, in which I can connect wholeheartedly with what is in front of me. I am happy with less. I fully enjoy what is. I am infusing my world with this pace. Less is more.

I intend to slow down my nervous system. Why? My body is asking me to do this. Being in a hurry to get things done is in my DNA. American culture reinforces it.

Changing my thinking and other important reminders

- I have enough time.

- I trust myself.

- My words have value.

- Anyone who hears what I have to say is blessed.

- I can be present and take the time to speak.

- I practice active listening. Active listening is full engagement and focus, without interrupting, being distracted and/or thinking of what to say in response.

- In a conversation, I will actively listen without formulating a reply in my head.

- There is more than enough time for people to hear and listen to me.

- I only need to say it once.

- I can speak at a relaxed speed and people will hear and listen to me.

- I respect people by giving my full attention when they are speaking to me.

- People give me their full attention when I am speaking to them.

- People in a conversation will actively listen to me.

- I will happily wait until the person who is talking is completely finished speaking, even pause before I respond.

- People will happily wait until I am finished speaking, even pause before responding to me.

- Be calm and present, even if the person I am conversing with is incapable of listening. Listen and hold space for them. Be polite and calm.

- Discern what you say to whom. If it doesn't feel right to share, then don't.

- Give advice only when it's asked for.

- I have more than enough time for work, play, and self-care.

- I have inner calm amid excitement and chaos.

- All is well.

How does "fast" show up in me?

- Shallow breathing in the upper part of my chest.

- Walking forward with my head leading.

- Fast talking trying to get everything I can say out in a breath.

- Repeating what I say, feeling like I am not heard.

- Eating fast.

- Indigestion.

- Upset stomach, bloating and gas.

- Hurrying through what I'm doing.

- Multitasking, trying to fit everything in, and doing multiple things at once.

- Forgetting where I put things.

- Unaligned posture.

- Tightness in my neck and shoulders.

- Tightness in my jaws.

- Tension.

- Aches and pains.

- Headaches.

- Feelings of anxiousness.

- Feeling disconnected and uncertain.

- Impulsivity.

- Nervous laughter.

- Interrupted night sleeping.

- Can't think straight.

- Feeling overwhelmed and confused.

- Worry if I don't get it done when I think it, I'll forget about doing it.

I have been in this process of slowing down my entire life, and there are still a few things left that I need to work on. My nervous system needs a deep breath and to feel the breath moving all through my body. I need to feel the flow of life moving through my entire body.

Steps to Slowing Down

Step 1: Be conscious of my breath. I have learned to breathe deeply into my whole body, through my nose into my chest, down through my solar plexus into my sacral area, filling up my entire body down to my feet, exhaling, and being in that space of peace.

Step 2: Be conscious of my posture. I have learned to stand up correctly. I reset my posture often by standing up, looking up to the ceiling, bringing my head down, pushing my chin back, rolling my shoulders back, and tucking my tailbone down. This is what I call "aligned posture." I have learned to walk with an aligned posture.

Step 3: Be mindful of what I do. I have been slowing down everything I do by being conscious of my actions. Do one thing at a time.

Step 4: Be mindful of my rate of speech. I am in the process of slowing down my speed of speech. I'm learning that if I don't have the space to slow down my speech, I will not speak.

Step 5: Be an active listener. When I listen, I am fully engaged. I focus on the speaker, listen with the heart with compassion and understanding

My plan for completely healing the rest of my nervous system is to be present, periodically check my breathing for depth, checking my posture for alignment, and always remembering to check the speed of my speech. I commit to this because my body is asking me to make this change for my nervous system so that I may continue to live a long and happy life. I release my nervous system to my breath. May it relax and release old patterns.

I apologize for passing this nervous system down to my descendants. The work I have done and am doing will help future generations.

5 Keys to a Functioning Nervous System

1. Breathe fully and deeply.
2. Train your mind to be still and focused.
3. Take care of your body. Listen to it.
4. Be compassionate to yourself and others.
5. Listen to your inner guidance: tune into balance, stop, and rest.

Moments of Living a Balanced Pace

- I took ample time in the morning to be still before jumping into my day.

- I broke down a project into smaller tasks, giving each task the attention it needed.

- I stopped when I felt like I had enough.

- I took my time and didn't hurry. When I find myself in a hurry, I stop and reassess. Am I doing too much? What needs to go?

- I was in a hurry to avoid being late for class, so I forgot to pay the parking meter. I found two tickets on my windshield.

- When I hurry, I am not present, space out, and need to remember things.

- I packed for a two-week trip.

Journal

How can you slow down your nervous system and find inner peace? Please reflect and answer the question.

Joyful Moments: Record your joyful moments. Let your heart express itself through art.

Week 47: Empowering Health through Choices

"All diseases begin in the gut."

—Hippocrates

Guidance: **Your body speaks to you through pain and discomfort.**

It is urging you on a journey towards better health and a lifestyle that supports your well-being. Remember that the memory of pain is a powerful reminder to avoid habits that harm your health. With awareness and conscious choices, you can protect and nurture your body. Avoiding foods that cause inflammation is easy because you have a lasting impression of pain that jumps out from your memory bank to remind you immediately. Just looking at the trigger food is enough of a reminder not to eat it.

Realization: **My gallbladder spoke to me through pain and inflammation.**

I had to make a change in the way I ate. I found it through trial and error. Now my diet focuses on reducing inflammation by eating foods that don't trigger inflammation in my gallbladder. Inflammation causes my liver to feel enlarged and gives me pain in my front and back in the liver region. My gallbladder diet gave me the power to control and regulate my eating experience.

I listened to and tracked my body's response to my food to create my diet. I then eliminated those foods that trigger a painful response. As I removed those foods, my gallbladder diet appeared. Through my eating journey and medical testing, I found I have an aging gallbladder that is slow to break down animal fat. I have no gallstones or sludge. Altering my diet and taking enzymes as needed have eliminated my gallbladder problems.

5 Keys to Empowering Health through Choices

1. Listen to your body.
2. Trial and error.
3. Track your body's response.
4. Empowerment through dietary control.
5. Seek medical advice.

Choosing Joyful Moments

- Painting with my granddaughter.
- Playing Rummikub with my grandchildren.
- Cooking with my grandson.
- Being a passenger in a four-wheeled-off road vehicle while my grandson drove me around.
- I was a passenger in the side-by-side while my granddaughter drove me around.
- Getting hugs from my grandchildren.
- Listening to my granddaughter as she taught me how to use bear spray.

Journal

What changes have you made to your diet to support your health? Please reflect and answer the question.

Joyful Moments: Record your joyful moments. Let your heart express itself through art.

Week 48: Self-Pacing

"Focus on your lane, go at your own pace, don't look sideways.

Someone else's success does not have to impact you or detract from what you achieve."

—Zoe Sugg

Guidance: **Proper planning will allow for pleasant memory-making.**

Think through the planned event. What do you need to support your health and equilibrium and have a wonderful experience? Do not do too much. Less is more. What can you cut out? What is just right? Ask for help. Think out of the box.

Ask for help. Think out of the box . . . Keep hydrated. Rest as needed.

Stop just before you've had enough—moderation in all things. Think Goldilocks. Not too little, not too much, just right.

Listen to your body's messages: pain, out of breath, racing heart, inflammation, and overheating. Wear proper clothing for weather and activity, as your body is more sensitive to the wind, sun and cold as you age. Dress for the weather. For example, wearing a hat or cover-up is essential to protect yourself from excessive sun exposure. Keep hydrated. Rest as needed.

Realization: Today, I graduated from physical therapy. No more hip problems!

Yay! I am walking pain-free. I have no pain climbing stairs. *Pacing is key.* My seventy-second year has shown that I must remember to listen to my body and pace myself. Now I allow it. No longer do I push or force myself. I found out that I was not listening to my body. I was making my body my slave. Well, my body rebelled. My body refused, tightened, and became inflamed. I ignored all these messages until my hip protested.

After nine months of pain and frustration, I started physical therapy. Towards the end of five weeks, I was feeling much better. But, as usual, I was not pacing myself. I went into "overdo" mode. I learned the hard way that overdoing doesn't work either. My left hip went on strike. My left femur dislocated from my hip.

> *I am still in the learning process. The first big step is to listen to my body.*

Another six weeks of physical therapy were required to recover from that injury. In the last six weeks, I started listening to my body. The memory of cracking sounds and the pain, nearly passing out, riding in the ambulance, spending the day in an Emergency Room, using a wheelchair and a cane, taking painkillers, and having slow, restrictive movement for over a week imprinted on my brain that I must listen to my body when it speaks to me. Eventually, I will learn to pace myself. Stop and rest. Know when I have done enough. I am still in the learning process. The first big step is to listen to my body.

I wonder why I didn't listen to my body. Somewhere, I was taught to push through pain and work harder. For the record, this was wrong for me to do in my seventies.

5 Keys to Self-Pacing

1. Listen to your body and pace yourself. Pay attention to your body's messages, such as pain, fatigue, or inflammation. Stop and rest when needed.

2. Focus on your lane and go at your own pace. Don't compare yourself to others or let their success detract from your achievements.

3. Practice moderation in all things. Find the right balance between doing too little and doing too much. Aim for a level of activity that is just right for you.

4. Make adjustments and improvements gradually. Start with your baseline activity level and gradually increase frequency, intensity, time, weight, or distance. Be comfortable with each adjustment before moving on to the next. Remember, progress is progress, no matter how small.

5. Avoid overdoing it. Don't push yourself to the point of exhaustion or injury. Learn to stop just before you've had enough.

Moments of Self-Pacing

- Being with younger friends, I made time to rest while my friends were active.

- While kayaking, we took several breaks from sitting and swam.

- I self-paced at the gym by stopping at a critical point.

- Driving home from Santa Fe, I stopped four times to stretch.

- I realize that sitting too long stiffens my body.

- I enjoy how my body feels when I get moving.

- I have more energy when I exert my entire body. The endorphins make a difference in how I feel about everything.

Journal

Have you ever experienced a time when you didn't listen to your body's signals and pushed yourself too hard? What were the consequences, and what did you learn from that experience? Please reflect and answer the questions.

Joyful Moments: Record your joyful moments. Let your heart express itself through art.

Week 49: Unleashing the Power of Transformation

"Smooth seas do not make skillful sailors."

—African Proverb

Guidance: Imagine a caterpillar transforming into a butterfly.

The process starts with the caterpillar in its cocoon. Within the cocoon, a significant change occurs. Have you ever seen the butterfly still encased in its cocoon? A metamorphosis is taking place. The structure of the caterpillar is broken down and used to form the butterfly. Eventually, the butterfly emerges from its cocoon, beautiful, no longer having the life of a caterpillar crawling on the ground. Instead, it spreads its wings and embraces a new existence.

Your transformational journey mirrors this metamorphosis, facilitating growth, change, and

Be open to all possibilities! Anything and Everything is possible!

evolution of consciousness. To reach your potential, choose to face challenges, let go of old patterns, and embrace new possibilities. Be open to all possibilities! Anything and everything is possible! Stay awake. The way will be shown to you. Don't be dismayed by what you see in the world. Don't resist, fight, or judge it. You are about something far greater. Everyone is. Everything you need will appear.

Realization: I only listen to my inner guidance, which guides me to shed my old cocoon mentality.

The urge to fix others is my old cocoon consciousness. When it shows up, I stop myself. My inner guidance protects and steers me away from paths that do not serve me, signaling me through my body's pain or discomfort. My inner guidance wants me to experience joy and freedom.

Having done my work, I am ready to heal. I am here to embody love, light, and joy. Mother Earth has witnessed atrocities for billions of years. She longs to see me living in harmony and happiness. Don't all mothers wish that for their children? Mother Earth conveyed to me that I have had enough sorrow.

My Light Daughter, Bonnie, said, "Mom, no more sorrow! There is nothing more you can do but experience the joys of life: Your children, your family, nature, the trees, the deer, dance and sing, and have fun! Do what sparks your joy. Remember, you can't fix anyone, but you can ruin your life trying. Everyone must do their work; you can't do it for them. You did your work. Let them do theirs.

"I love you. You are doing the best you can. The Divine Mother loves you. You are perfect, just as you are. Accept people just as they are. Then, you will begin to see the magic of life. All your life's problems will dissipate. Everything is perfect, just as it is. Your life has been perfectly designed and orchestrated for you. There is no other like you. In nature, there is diversity, not duplicates. As you become aware, what you thought were 'problems' magically become blessings. The mind struggles to comprehend it. It can't. A higher intelligence is at work. The mind learns to know its place, to serve 'inner guidance.' A perfect life has been given to you allowing you to learn what you need to be free to fly and be the butterfly you are."

My responsibility is to maintain a clear line of love and communication with my partner, my children, my family, my friends, nature, and the land where I live. I am now on the path of joy, a joyful journey that is mine to pursue. That's enough. When they see me happy and radiant, they will feel it, too. I trust that.

5 Keys to Transformation

1. Embrace the Process of Transformation.
2. Trust Your Inner Guidance.
3. Release the Need to Fix Others.
4. Embrace Joy and Lightness.
5. Cultivate Clear Communication and Love.

Mission Statement for My Transformation

Having a clear mission statement delivers clarity and direction for the future.

My mission is to live joyfully as an alive, passionate, centered woman with the energy and the physical and mental ability to have fun with my family and friends. At the same time, I learn, grow, and contribute to my world.

My Vision to Implement My Mission

I have deliberately written my vision statement in the present tense to create it in the now.

Alive - I'm fully alive and engaged. I choose to be helpful, creative, and joyful.

Centered - I actively maintain a pure heart.

Joyful - My sense of humor lightens and brightens my world. I find humor in everyday situations and laugh often.

Physical Ability: I treat my body with love and respect and strive to keep it healthy, flexible, and responsive. I understand the importance of knowing when to rest and stop.

Mental Ability - My mind and memory are sharp and quick. My decision-making is based on wisdom and experience.

Creativity - I express my feelings and thoughts creatively through writing, art, and movement.

Fun with Family and Friends- We share, play, and celebrate our lives.

Learn - I'm curious, interested in, and passionate about learning.

Contribute to My World - I contribute to my world by understanding and using my gifts and talents to make a positive impact. I do what is mine to do.

Journal

You are invited to write your mission statement. How can embracing transformation and cultivating joy lead to personal growth and self-discovery? Please reflect and answer the question. Let your heart express itself through art.

Joyful Moments: Record your joyful moments. Let your heart express itself through art.

Week 50: Finding Joy Within Meditation

"When we are mindful, deeply in touch with the present moment, our understanding of what is going on deepens, and we begin to be filled with acceptance, joy, peace and love."

—Thich Nhat Hanh

Guidance: **Mindfulness is a primary strategy for maintaining health and well-being.**

Remember to practice mindfulness while eating, moving, resting, expressing, reflecting, and responding to life's challenges. It's a wonder remedy for what ails you. It gives you the ability to appreciate what is.

Mindfulness is being in the present moment. Mindfulness is meditation. It can be done throughout the day. Thoughts may move through like clouds. When the thoughts tell a story and take you out of the present moment, focus on your breathing. Tell your mind you will look at this later during a specific meditative time. Your mind can be like an untrained dog that needs direction, attention and kind discipline. Speak to it with understanding and love. Then continue in your Zen moment.

Later, during quiet sitting or lying down uninterrupted intentional meditation, you can address what is going on in your mind, you can observe it and see what it is and where it comes from. It is not you but a pattern that has been reinforced throughout your life when dealing with things. It could be your child self, mother self, firefighter self or an old fear or pattern. . . understand it. Love it and show compassion. Breathe through it. Break the habitual pattern response. Relax, feel at ease, feel safe, and feel better informed.

Eventually, you are no longer controlled by unconscious reactions to the unfettered mind. This process helps deal with grief, loss, anxiety, and everything else in life.

Realization: I can only speak for myself.

I continually see that everything within and outside my world needs my love and compassion. I am connected to everything.

As I love the dysfunction and forgive myself and my ancestors who played a role in creating it, my world is lifted. These are hard, unbearable times for many. So much injustice, hate, and sorrow have been revealed. There is great sadness. Humankind can no longer live separated from their higher power. I keep my eyes and heart on the truth of love. Miraculously, things that once seemed fixed in concrete are transforming. I know I came on Earth for this time. What is true for me is true for you.

Guided Meditation

I am a teacher, not a therapist or medical professional. I designed this meditation as a teaching tool. Its objective is to help the listener find joy within. First, read the entire meditation. The entire meditation is on YouTube. This is not a substitute for medical attention and care. Please seek professional help when you need it.

You will have ample time for this experience. At the end of this 25-minute journey, your time is up, and you will return to your regular activity. Have writing material or a recorder ready so you can record what you experience.

Finding Joy Within Meditation

Welcome to this guided meditation on finding joy within. Find a comfortable position, either sitting or lying down. Close your eyes and notice your breath. Breathe normally. Watch your breath slow down. Take three deep breaths. Relax as you scan your body from the top of your head to the bottom of your feet and release any tension.

You are going on a journey to nurture and cultivate joy within yourself. Throughout this meditation, I will guide you as you explore different aspects of joy and invite its presence into your life.

Now, focus on your breath. Notice the gentle rhythm of your breath as it flows in and out of your body. Imagine breathing in positive energy and releasing negativity or tension with each exhale.

Invite the feeling of joy into your body. As you explore joy, notice the sensations within your body. Pay attention to any feelings of warmth, flow, tingling, lightness, or expansion. They are signs of joy manifesting within you. Feel. Allow a deep breath to fill your lower belly, slowly relaxing as you release it.

If your thoughts drift, gently bring your attention to the present moment. Anchor your awareness in the sensation of your breath or your body. Remember, this is a practice, and each time you focus on the present moment, you strengthen your ability to find joy. Approach this practice with an open mind, a sense of curiosity, and a willingness to explore. Allow joy to be your guide as you embark on this inner journey.

Imagine yourself in a place that brings you great joy and inner peace. It could be a serene beach, a vibrant garden, a grove of trees, a meadow of flowers, or any other place that resonates with you.

Visualize this setting in vivid detail, including the time of day, the sun's position, lighting, colors, hues, lines, and shapes.

Listen for the sounds. It could be birds singing, leaves whispering, gentle waves caressing the ocean shore, or whatever comes to you. Allow your imagination to bring it to life.

As you immerse yourself in this joyful place, fully experience the positive feelings that arise—happiness, gratitude, peace, and contentment—as your heart opens and fills with them. Let these feelings expand and radiate throughout your entire being, soaking in the beauty and joy that surrounds you.

You notice something: a beautiful radiant light that embodies joy. Joy transforms into a form that you know and love. What form does it take? Joy wants to be your friend. Let joy speak to you, listen to its messages, and follow its guidance.

Silence for 5 minutes. How does your body feel? Joy is now within you and accessible at any time. As you near the end of this meditation, reflect on the joy you have discovered within yourself. Recognize that joy is always available, no matter the circumstances, residing in your heart and expanding through mindfulness and gratitude.

Now, it is time to return to the present reality of the room you are in. Wiggle your toes and fingers. Gently move your body. When you are ready, open your eyes, giving your attention to the present moment. Throughout the day, notice the joy found in simple things—nature's beauty, the sun's warmth on your skin, or the sound of laughter in the distance. Find joy in the small moments that often go unnoticed and carry this sense of joy with you as you return to the world around you. Please write down what comes to your mind now.

5 Keys to Finding Joy Within Meditation

1. Notice the sensations within your body.
2. Anchor your awareness in the present moment.
3. Approach meditation with an open mind and curiosity.
4. Visualize a joyful place.
5. Reflect on the joy within yourself.

Joyful Moments

- I felt satisfied. My grandson is heading to college in the fall. He has his housing all set.
- I was excited about our travel day tomorrow. A sure sign of this is when I can't find my keys and other things.

- I felt relieved when I found a misplaced number I was looking for.
- I felt relieved when I found my travel backpack hidden in the loft.
- I felt relaxed after twenty minutes of meditation.
- I felt organized. I have hard copies of all our Alaska travel arrangements.
- I felt peace knowing I had taken care of everything I could think of for our travel day tomorrow.

Journal

How did your perception of joy change or deepen as you immersed yourself in the meditation? What images did joy take on for you during the meditation, and how did these forms resonate with you? How can you incorporate mindfulness and gratitude into your routine to help expand your experience of joy?

Joyful Moments: Reflect and freely write from your heart about your weekly joy experience or any insights you may have. Let your heart express itself through art.

Week 51: Embracing Personal Responsibility and Boundaries in Relationships

"Responsibility is not only about what we do but also about setting and respecting boundaries."

—Oprah Winfrey

Guidance: Setting and maintaining personal boundaries is essential in a world of demands and limitations.

Here's a simplified approach:

Step 1: Know your boundaries. Understand that you have the right to define your boundaries. Some people may naturally pick up on them.

Step 2: If Step 1 doesn't work, calmly communicate your boundaries using "I statements." Avoid anger, blame, or meanness. People are more likely to listen when you approach them with respect.

Step 3: Be consistent and clear in communicating your boundaries. Please keep it simple. Things may temporarily worsen before they improve. Stay calm and non-emotional.

Step 4: Remember that your past behaviors have influenced how others treat you. You can teach others how you want to be treated by setting and enforcing boundaries.

Step 5: Understand that the other person is not the problem. If their behavior bothers you, it's your responsibility to address it. Avoid complaining. Change begins with you. Approach all of this with love for yourself and the other person.

Step 6: The other person may distance themselves from your life.

Even in this situation, you can still love them while their behavior no longer affects you. Love them from a distance.

Realization: I need to understand that I cannot solve other people's problems or provide happiness for them.

I am responsible for my own life and the actions I take. I need to recognize that my anguish, anxiety, and stress do not help anyone else but rather exacerbate my issues. When I take personal responsibility for my emotions and well-being, I create a space for joy to enter my life. While I may feel an instinct to care for and fix things for my loved ones, I must understand they have the resources and capabilities to solve their problems. My role is to support, love, and encourage my loved ones. It is up to them to find their happiness and make their own decisions. By letting go of the need to control others' happiness, I can experience true joy. I create healthier and more balanced relationships when I stop carrying others' responsibilities, guilt, or faults.

It's not my purpose in life to be everything to everyone, and by releasing myself from this pressure, I allow others to grow and take responsibility for their own lives. This sense of freedom and empowerment brings immense joy into my life. I activate joy by embracing personal responsibility and understanding the boundaries in my relationships. I create a space to focus on my growth and well-being while supporting and empowering others to do the same. This balance and alignment with my own needs and the needs of others bring a deep sense of joy and fulfillment to my life.

5 Keys to Developing Your Boundaries

1. Understand that you cannot solve other people's problems or provide happiness for them.

2. Take responsibility for your own life and actions, recognizing that your anguish, anxiety, and stress do not help others.

3. Take personal responsibility for your emotions and well-being, creating space for joy in your life.

4. Recognize that your loved ones have the resources and capabilities to solve their problems.

5. Support, love, and encourage your loved ones, but understand that it is ultimately up to them to find their happiness and make their own decisions.

Journal

Reflect on your boundaries and responsibilities in life. How did this week's reading challenge your preconceived notions and broaden your understanding of the world? Please reflect and answer the questions.

Joyful Moments: Reflect and freely write from your heart about your weekly joy experience or any insights you may have. Let your heart express itself through art.

Week 52: An Ideal Day

"Every day is a new opportunity to create an ideal day. It's not about waiting for perfect circumstances but about making the most of what we have. Embrace each moment, find joy in the little things, and make every day count."

—Oprah Winfrey

Guidance: Plan to make the most of your experiences.

Be open to new opportunities for growth. Be adaptable and give space to let creative solutions emerge. Eat healthy food and take care of yourself. Connect with the people you meet and be grateful for each day. By doing these things, you can transform your days into joyful experiences.

Realization: I can always turn lemons into lemonade.

No matter what happens, every day is ideal from beginning to end. Every day holds the potential to be ideal. It is up to us to embrace this mindset and make the most of each precious moment. Imagine, just for a day, approaching every experience with a sense of wonder and gratitude. Try it and see the transformation it brings.

As I awaken each morning, I express gratitude for the opportunities and blessings that lie ahead. By having a mindset of appreciation, I invite more joy into my life. I take a moment to acknowledge beauty, the simple pleasures that often go unnoticed, and the endless possibilities that await.

By cultivating a mindset of appreciation, we invite more joy into our lives.

Throughout the day, I practice being fully present in each moment. I engage wholeheartedly in whatever task or activity I am involved in. By paying attention to the details and savoring the experiences, I enhance my enjoyment and find fulfillment in the simplest things. Be immersed in the present, letting go of worries about the past or the future.

A quote on my mirror reminds me of my mission, which aligns with my goals, values, and aspirations. This positive affirmation encourages me to affirm my worth and potential, boosts my confidence, and attracts positive outcomes. I believe in the limitless possibilities each day holds and watch my dreams unfold effortlessly. Then, the belief becomes a knowing.

Life will inevitably present unexpected changes and challenges. Instead of resisting or becoming overwhelmed, I welcome them with an open mind and a flexible attitude. I see them as opportunities for growth and learning, steppingstones to my ideal day. I embrace the lessons they offer and adapt gracefully to the obstacles that come my way.

Above all, I prioritize self-care activities that nourish my mind, body, and heart. I make time for exercise, meditation, nature walks, hobbies, and meaningful connections with loved ones. Taking care of myself replenishes my energy and fosters a positive mindset. I fill up on self-love.

5 Keys to an Ideal Day

1. Gratitude.
2. Mindfulness.
3. Positive affirmations.
4. Flexibility.
5. Self-care.

Moments of Ideal Day at Lake Powell

- The boat we rented had steering problems. Three different times the mechanic came to our rescue. It is what it is. The mechanics were surprised and thankful for how gracious and understanding we were.

- Hiked to Rainbow Bridge.

- Kayaked a beautiful winding cove.

- At 8:30 p.m., the winds picked up and riled the waters. With only two anchors, one anchor became loose, and the other could not do its job. In all our previous experiences with houseboats, we always had four anchors. Now we know why. Anchors dragged into the lake bottom. The crewless boat drifted. The ropes got caught in the motors and lost the boat plank. We returned the boat to shore. Secured both anchors. *Que sera, sera.* Around 10:30 p.m. things were under control.

- Found plank. Reattached to boat.

- Snorkeled in the lake.

- Took photos of light on the waters.

How can it get any better than this? John and the other seasoned sailors took expert action. It was quite a team effort! Following John's leadership, we were all engaged. We deepened our friendship. Thanks, heaven, for natural adrenalin uptake.

Journal

What made today an ideal day? Reflect and answer the question.

Joyful Moments: Reflect and freely write from your heart about your weekly joy experience or any insights you may have. Let your heart express itself through art.

Incante: Realm of Beauty and Light

"The body is the vehicle for the soul's incarnation,
allowing us to experience life's beauty and purpose."

—Maya Angelou

Dear Ones:

In our previous considerations in Weeks 11 and 17, John and I
delved into presence and vibrational energy. However, I understand
that the mind can sometimes confuse these concepts. I intend
to have you feel your vibrational energy. This guided meditation
provides an opportunity to connect with your vibrational energy.
You will be transported to an imaginary realm, Incante (YouTube),
whose atmosphere permeates sacred energy. "Incante" is derived
from the Italian word "incanto" meaning enchantment. It represents a realm of beauty and light that captivates the heart. I hope
this journey will allow you to experience sacred vibrational energy
and connect with the vastness of the universe.

With love and light,
Anita

As you go on this mystical journey, allow all your senses to
experience it viscerally. I have found that when I did this journey,
my body, mind, and heart recall this place's peace and sacredness.

Whatever your experience in meditation, remember you will
receive what is just right for you.

Suggestions on how to engage with this meditation:

- Read this entire meditation.

- Have someone read this meditation to you.

- Listen to my Incante YouTube video.
- Watch my Incante YouTube video.

Narrator:

1. Remember to breathe into the words as you read this guided meditation.

2. Take time with each sentence, pausing at the prepositional phrases and commas and stopping at periods. Allow for silence.

3. After each paragraph, reflect on the words you just heard.

Introduction

You are going on an imaginary journey to an enchanting place. I like to think of it as a recharge, where we plug into the outlet of Divine Light. I have named this place Incante, the realm of Divine Beauty and Light. On this journey, there is no need to fear the unknown, for we are always safe and protected in the hands of the Divine. If you feel uneasy, remind yourself, "I am safe." As you listen to my voice, allow your imagination to create images. It is like directing your movie in the theater of your mind, where you are the star. At the end of the journey, I will softly say, "Dear ones," and you will return to the ordinary reality.

Whether you are seated or lying down, make yourself comfortable. Take a moment to check in with your body. Do you need a blanket or a pillow? When you feel ready, gently close your eyes.

Breathing

Open your heart. Connect with the Net of Light. Let's breathe together. We will initiate the energy for our journey with the 4:8 breathing practice:

Inhale for a count of four: one, two, three, four.

Exhale for a count of eight: one, two, three, four, five, six, seven, eight.

Again, *inhale* for a count of four: one, two, three, four.

Exhale for a count of eight: one, two, three, four, five, six, seven, eight.

One last time, *inhale* for a count of four: one, two, three, four.

Exhale for a count of eight: one, two, three, four, five, six, seven, eight. And now, let us begin the journey.

Your attention is drawn to a tall evergreen tree with markings on its bark. Curious, you decide to investigate. Imagine you are deep in the forest, surrounded by the sounds of nature. Picture the scenery, perhaps the birds singing and the deer grazing on the grass. Feel the gentle breeze and warm sunlight. How does your body feel?

In an instant, you find yourself directly facing the tree trunk. The markings you saw from a distance are steps in the trunk and are part of a staircase that leads towards the sky. Slowly, you ascend, feeling the sturdy support of the tree beneath your feet. Each step feels safe and trustworthy. One by one, you climb effortlessly until you reach the top. You take a moment to look down and marvel at the breathtaking view. Turning to the sky above, you see a canvas of colors and swirling clouds. The air is filling you with a sense of aliveness. As you gaze upward,

The light of the sun shines directly on your face, momentarily blinding you. As you take a deep breath in, you are lifted. Up into the clouds, higher and higher, from cloud to cloud, transcending the earthly realm. Finally, you arrive at Incante.

You followed the light. The current of your breath brought you here. As you awaken from this dreamlike state, you feel a shift in energy. Your eyes widen as you behold the splendor of the landscape. Your heart fills with awe and wonder. You are beyond the limitations of your human experience. Take a moment to soak in the beauty that surrounds you. Feel the energy in your body. What do you feel?

Time ceases to exist in the celestial realm of Incante. Every moment is eternal. Worries or concerns don't exist. The energy here is pure and harmonious and resonates with joy. How does it feel in your body?

Celestial beings, radiant with light, surround you in every direction. They are your guides on this journey, showering you with love and wisdom. Their presence brings peace and clarity. They illuminate your path. What do they look like? How are they dressed? How do you feel when you are with them? Take a moment to connect with each of your guides and feel their loving energy envelope you.

You have connected with universal consciousness, connecting with something greater than yourself. This realm is filled with unlimited possibilities and the infinite. Here, life is created through the merging of light and love. This place goes beyond known words. This place is extraordinary and mystical. Here the boundaries of the known dissolve. Think universal consciousness. What do you feel? In your heart? In your body?

You are ready to explore Incante. There is so much to see. "Where do I start?" No sooner than the thought crosses your mind than a path lights up and standing before you are your light guides shining the way. No struggles in Incante. If you think it, "it happens instantaneously."

Your guides lead you through the Divine Gardens. You see flowers of every color and shape. The air is filled with the sweet scent of blossoms. The gentle sound of trickling water from nearby streams creates a melody. As you walk through the gardens, feel the vibrant energy of life pulsating through every living thing. What does it feel like?

In this moment of connection, ask the universe one question you may have or seek guidance on a particular aspect of your life. Trust that the answer will come through intuitive thoughts, feelings, or symbols, now or when you are back in ordinary reality. Allow yourself to be open and receptive to the universe's messages.

Take a moment to receive the guidance and wisdom offered to you. Feel the love and support of the universe surrounding you, empowering you to embrace your highest potential and live a life aligned with your true purpose.

In the distance, a majestic waterfall cascades down from a towering cliff. Approach the waterfall and feel its cool mist on your skin. The positive ions revitalize your senses. How does your body feel now?

A shimmering pond at the base of the waterfall draws your attention. Its crystal-clear waters reflect the brilliance of the sky above. Dip your hand into the water and feel its gentle caress. Gaze into the pond's depths and glimpse your true essence, your inner light shining brightly. What do you realize about your true nature?

You come upon the wellspring of truth, and a ladle rests on the edge of the spring. Take it, dip it into the spring, lift the ladle to your mouth, and drink. Feel refreshed as the energy moves through your being, awakening unknown parts of you. Unleash the power of truth within you. Lying down by the wellspring, you discover the depths of your true nature. What is the power of your true nature? Allow yourself to assimilate all this new awareness.

Having integrated the new experience of yourself, you are ready to move on. Just beyond the wellspring, there is a cave. You wander freely into the cave, and a voice calls, "Come closer. Hidden treasures lie within." It is your radiant companions. You trust your guides as you wander into the cave. You hear, "Be still. Find your still point; your treasures will be revealed to you. You are free to explore and discover. Let the light guide you on your journey of self-discovery." The cave is a place of transformation and growth where you can release limitations and further open to your full potential. Just go within. Discover hidden gems inside you. Be open to the magic and wonder surrounding you. What hidden gems did you discover?

Venture further into Incante and welcome the unknown with an open heart. Here, you come alive and find your purpose. The possibilities in Incante are endless. This state of being is familiar to you; you feel like you have returned to your true home. Your spirit soars in the realm of Incante, and you feel a deep sense of belonging and connection. You know your true identity. What is the truth of your identity?

Your whole being expresses your love and gratitude to the Source of All. You feel deep gratitude for everything you've just experienced. Gratitude for what you know. Gratitude for knowing who you are and the truth of yourself. Gratitude washes over you, through you and seeps into every cell of your body. You will never forget that a pure heart is ever grateful.

The Light Guides say, "You feel lighter and more aligned with your true purpose. Carry the essence of Incante with you; know it will guide and inspire you on your earthly journey. The new light in your eyes will appreciate beauty and tranquility. Infuse love and joy into every aspect of your life. You can access any part of this journey when you are back in ordinary reality. Initiate the energy of Incante with the 4:8 breathing practice. You think of the cave and be there. You can think of the wellspring and be there. You can think of the pond and be there. Think about any part of your journey, and you'll be there—no need to go to the forest and climb stairs.

It is time to return to your earth's reality. Your Light guides help you rapidly retrace your footsteps: cave, wellspring, pond, waterfall, garden; depart Incante; clouds, platform: tree trunk staircase, forest, ordinary reality. The narrator softly speaks, "Dear One." Now, slowly bring your awareness back to your physical surroundings. Wiggle your fingers and toes, allowing yourself to become fully present. When you are ready, gently open your eyes, carrying the magic of Incante as you continue your life journey.

Namaste

A suggestion: Before I sleep at night, I feel the essence of Incante. On the inhale, I feel the words, "Breathe In-Can-te." (four breaths) On the exhale, I think, "I give my concerns to the Light" (eight breaths). You might want to try it. You can substitute your own words to fit the breathing pattern.

5 Keys to Finding Incante

1. Connect with your vibrational energy: Feel your vibrational energy and connect with it. This is the first step to finding Incante.

2. Follow the guided meditation: The provided guided meditation takes you on a journey to Incante. You can access the realm of Beauty and Light by following the meditation.

3. Ascend the staircase: In the meditation, you face a tree trunk with markings that are steps leading toward the sky. Ascending these stairs will take you closer to Incante.

4. Marvel at the view and feel the energy: When you reach the top of the staircase, take a moment to look down and marvel at the view below. Feel the power of the vastness of the universe and the vibrational energy in your body.

5. Connect with celestial beings and universal consciousness. Feel their loving energy. Also, connect with universal consciousness and feel the expansiveness within your heart and body.

Journal

Write about your vibrational energy and the expansiveness of higher consciousness in your heart and body. Reflect on the insight and revelations you received during your time in the realm of Incante.

Joyful Moments: Reflect and write freely from your heart about the joyful experience or any insights you may have. Let your heart express itself through art.

CONCLUSION

"It's not about being perfect. It's not about where you get yourself in the end.

There's power in allowing yourself to be known and heard, in owning your unique story,

in using your authentic voice."

—Michelle Obama

Guidance: I understand that you are on an internal journey. I know that, at times, you may not feel joy. It's okay to feel that way.

Even though you may not know where you are going, remember that you are not lost. It's like you are blind and feeling each step along the way, and that's completely okay. You are walking on a path that is wide enough for you to move freely. When you get to the edge of it, say you lose yourself in a thought. You begin to knock into something. You feel something. Refrain from translating it as something terrible and become angry, fearful, guilty, jealous, resentful, or whatever. Remind yourself of the path that you are on. Feel your breath, trust, and visualize the path. Breathe, relax. You are back on it, back in the present moment. It's as easy as that. Always, it is as easy as that!

If you need help when you are way out there, you will have work to do. That's okay. This is your learning process on Earth. There is no judgment or shame. As you know, staying aware of the breath takes discipline and retraining. Forgive yourself. Forgive others. You still have much to learn. There is no shame or guilt in making mistakes. Learn from them.

> *There is no shame or guilt in making mistakes. Learn from them.*

Realization: I am committed to my journey of joy.

As we close this transformative chapter, I feel a tinge of sadness, but trust all is unfolding as it should. I'd love to hear how your life has transformed—please send me a brief update.

The lessons, insights, and experiences we've shared have woven a tapestry of wholeness and interconnectedness. Through our entire journey, we've unlocked a more harmonious way of being. We've learned to listen to our hearts, honor life's cycles, and see the divine in all creation.

This journey has challenged us, but in adversity we've discovered our greatest strengths and resilience. We've embraced grief, transmuted emotions into wisdom, and trusted the unfolding present.

As we move forward, may we carry these lessons into our daily lives. May we continue finding joy, balance, and deep connection to the world. We are part of a web of life, working together to create a more beautiful, loving world.

Much love, Anita

GLOSSARY

All In – Fully engaged without doubt.

Applied Attunement - Refers to living from a place of mindfulness and being in harmony with Love and Light in my life.

Attunement - A non-touch practice of connecting with the inner vibration of Light and Love. Using my hands, this energy flows through the Endocrine System, facilitating self-healing and balance.

Ancestors of Light - This represents my spiritual connection and guidance from my ancestors, extending beyond my biological family members.

Celestial Realms - The unseen, spiritual dimensions or planes of existence beyond the physical world that I explore.

Emissaries of Divine Light – A spiritual organization focused on attunement and personal and collective transformation.

Energetic Attunement - Aligning my personal energy field with a higher vibrational frequency or consciousness.

Grandmother - The loving, wise, and playful matriarch who embodies qualities who embodies love.

Ho'oponopono - A centuries-old native Hawaiian method of apology for reconciliation and forgiveness involving the phrases "I'm sorry, please forgive me, thank you, I love you."

Indra's Net - An ancient Hindu and Buddhist philosophy metaphor describing the universe as a vast, interconnected web where each node reflects all the others.

Net of Light - Also known as the "Web of Light" or "Cosmic Web," this refers to an energetic grid or light matrix connecting all of life and consciousness.

Oneness - The understanding that all of existence is fundamentally interconnected and that there is no actual separation between self and other.

Presence - A state of being fully engaged and aware in the present moment, without my mind being distracted by the past or future.

Reiki - A Japanese energy healing practice that promotes physical, mental, and emotional well-being by channeling universal life force energy.

Serendipity - My term for the meaningful coincidences that occur in life, seen as divinely endowed.

Singing Bowls - These crystal quartz bowls produce a rich, reverberating tone when chimed or rubbed with a soft mallet, used for meditation and energy work.

Spirit Net - Another term used to describe the interconnected, energetic matrix that underlies all of existence.

Synchronicity - The experience of two or more seemingly unrelated events that occur in a meaningful coincidence in my life.

The Grandmothers - An aspect of God that opened me to a new personal understanding of the Divine.

Threshold Choir - A community of singers who provide comfort and solace through music at the bedsides of those nearing the end of life.

Vibrational Energy - The understanding that all matter and energy in the universe is in a constant state of vibration, with each element having its unique frequency or "vibration."

Web of Life - A metaphor for the interdependence and interconnectedness of all living things in the natural world.

Yin and Yang - The complementary principles in Chinese philosophy represent the feminine (Yin) and masculine (Yang) energies that make up the natural world and human experience.

ACKNOWLEDGMENTS

I express my heartfelt gratitude to my dear husband, John Albright, Sr. John contributed significantly to this book. I recorded our dialogues, and the substance of his spiritual insights is woven throughout the book. This book would not have become a reality without his support, encouragement, input, and editing expertise. His belief in my ability to write this book gave me the confidence to complete it.

Bonnie Jeanne Albright, my Light Daughter, deserves special mention for her guidance and inspiration. Her presence, wisdom, and encouragement have been instrumental in shaping the essence of this book. Her contribution has added great value to the content and has inspired me throughout this journey. All profits from this book will be donated to the Bonnie J. Albright Fort Lewis College Teacher Education Scholarship Fund.

I extend my love and gratitude to my four children, who have stood by me and encouraged me to grow and find happiness again. I appreciate my son, John Jr, my daughter, Sabina, and all my family, who encouraged me to write my story.

I am grateful for all the love and joy I have received from my nine grandchildren. When I am with them, I can't help but focus on the joy in the moment.

A special acknowledgment goes to my grief counselor, who helped me realize that I deserve to be happy and live life fully. She directed me to Mindful Meditation.

I am forever grateful to Axis Health Systems, who provided instruction in Mindful Meditation, which made me aware that I was the observer of my suffering mother self.

I feel deep heartfelt gratitude to the Grandmothers and the Net of Light.

I am particularly grateful for Sharon McErlane and her Grandmothers books.

I appreciate the opportunity during the COVID pandemic, which connected me to global communities through Zoom. I value each of these Zoom groups: Forever Families, Net of Light, Keala O Kalani Hawaiian Ho'oponopono, Michael McQuade's Kentucky Families Anonymous, Safe Peace, Attunement Summits and Long Breathing.

In creating this book, I received invaluable support, guidance, and dedication from many individuals. While it is impossible to name each person, their contributions through feedback, encouragement, and assistance have made a meaningful impact on this journey.

SUGGESTED READINGS
FOR FURTHER STUDY

Books by Families Anonymous

Books by Irene Weinberg

Books by Jeffrey Goldstein

Books by Jon Kabat-Zinn

Books by Lloyd Meeker Sr.

Books by Martin Exeter

Books by Mary D'Agostino

Books by Pema Chodron

Books by Sharon McErlane

Books by Tara Bach

Books by Thich Nhat Hanh

Books Recommended by Forever Family Foundation

ABOUT THE AUTHOR

 Anita Albright, BA, MA, is a wife, mother, and grandmother on a lifelong journey of integrity and personal growth. With over thirty-two years of experience in teaching, Anita has educated students from various backgrounds and abilities, including those with dyslexia, autism spectrum disorders, and emotional and behavioral challenges. She firmly believes in teaching through experiential learning, making education a fun and engaging experience. Anita holds a BA in Psychology and Elementary Education and an MA in Special Education: Mild to Moderate Needs. She has also received extensive training in multisensory teaching methods.

In retirement, Anita continues to contribute to her community. She serves on the board of SW Colorado ARC. She also practices mindful meditation, energy work, and singing bowls. Anita's hobbies include writing, art, gardening, and time spent in nature. You can contact Anita at thankfulgrandma.blog or thankfulgrandma9@gmail.com. Meditations and travel videos can be found on YouTube: https://youtube.com/@thankfulgrandma9

Fort Lewis College Foundation
Support the Bonnie Albright Scholarship Fund!

Help FLC Foundation support students enrolled in teacher education! Created in memory of Bonnie Albright.

Join Anita's "Joyful Moments" Public Facebook Group

Follow "Journey to Joy" on Facebook

www.ingramcontent.com/pod-product-compliance
Lightning Source LLC
Chambersburg PA
CBHW021223130626
46554CB00004B/1334